I believe that women have an innate ability to reach the heart. In doing so they can lead people to Christ in a very genuine and honest way. I think the enemy believes this too, and he is going to do everything he can to distract women from this call. I also believe that God has called me to wake women up to who they really are. The more women I can wake up the more people can get saved. If I can wake ten and they can each wake ten, the possibilities are endless. There is no reason a single person should go to hell. And there is no reason any woman should enter heaven without having reached her full potential in Christ.

I want women to know that God has created them with unique gifts. He loves them so very much, just as they are. And He wants to reach the world through them. They too can reach the world for Jesus. They too can pour into the lives of others and rescue people from hell. I also want them to know that crappy stuff is going to happen. There will be trial and tragedy, frustration and pain, but these things do not define them. In fact, they can propel them into the life God has planned for them...if they allow them to. He wants to use it all for His glory.

He has anointed them to proclaim the good news to the poor
To bind up the broken hearted
To proclaim freedom for captives
And release from darkness
To comfort those who mourn
And provide for those who grieve
To give them a crown of beauty instead of ashes
The oil of joy instead of mourning
Praise instead of despair
To tell them that they will be called oaks of righteousness
The planting of the Lord for the display of his splendor

Relentlessly pursuing The King,

Libbie Hall

We don't really know what the future holds. We have hopes and dreams, but there's so much that is really so far beyond our control. Sometimes God will give us a glimpse of what is to come. Sometimes it's good and sometimes...it's not.

CHAPTER ONE

I was attending a prayer breakfast in early December of 2015 as a guest of my friend who owns a business in our area. I actually sit at her table every year. The speakers are always excellent. This particular year a woman by the name of Carol Kent shared her story, and it was heart-wrenching. Her son had married a woman with two precious daughters. They had become like Carol's own grandchildren. Their biological father had been accused of molesting them and they hadn't seen him in quite some time. Suddenly the family was faced with the reality that the man accused of such horrific acts was going to be granted visitation with the girls once again. In a moment of panic, Carol's son took matters into his own hands and shot and killed the girls' father. He was given a life sentence without the possibility of parole. The story from there is one of redemption and strength, much like that of Paul's. He chose to live for Jesus and his life was transformed. But Paul's life was never easy. This man, Carol's son, now runs a prison ministry from inside the prison. Hundreds of men's lives have been forever changed by this one man's dedication to Christ. But certainly, Carol would change the story if she could. Surely, there must be another way for God to be glorified in this. Yet Carol trusts God. She prays, accepting where they are now, believing for a miracle.

As I sat and listened to Carol's story I felt the Holy Spirit whispering to me that I would face a similar struggle...that my own son, Branden, would be arrested in the coming days. I tried to convince myself it wasn't God I was hearing, "It's just me being paranoid". I thought, "Not everything is about me!"

After the event, I stood in line to purchase Carol's book, "Laying my Isaac Down". I rushed to my car and put the book in the pouch behind the driver's seat...where it stayed...for a long time. On the way home I cried. I begged God to do something, to save Branden before he was to be arrested. To tell me I was imagining things. Days turned into months and everything seemed to go on as normal. I homeschooled my two younger children, led worship on Sundays, read my Bible and prayed. Perhaps I had just imagined it. Perhaps God wasn't preparing my heart for anything at all.

April rolled around and the sun was shining as I drove home from work at the church. Spring was beginning to break through the long hard winter. I was singing along with the Christian radio station when Bluetooth interrupted to tell me I had a call. It was my ex-husband, Branden's father. My heart sank, I knew the call wasn't just to say hello. The voice on the other end was almost apologetic, sad at the least...Branden had been arrested a few nights before. He was in jail awaiting a hearing. There it was, like the first bubbling of a volcano preparing to erupt. I felt it in the pit of my stomach, a warning that shouted, "Buckle up...things are about to get rocky."

But honestly, there is not a seatbelt in the world that could have prepared me for what I would experience. No one could have known. No one could have stopped it. Initially, the details of his arrest were sketchy. They unfolded slowly over the next eight months as I moved through the hearings and legal appointments that ensued. Time seemed to drag on, it was like those movies where the person is at a standstill but the world is flying by all around them. I was faced with a reality that life goes on in the midst of our tragedies. I mean, I knew this to be true, but I guess it had become a distant truth between my own personal tragedies.

Early on in the process, Branden called to say he had been moved to the Wayne County Jail for the duration of his hearing, so my husband reluctantly took me to see him. I can assure you, there is really no way to prepare for seeing your child behind bars. Everything about that visit was cold and hard. We were screened at security to ensure we didn't have any weapons or drugs on us. Once through we were given a paper pass and told to return to the desk within 50 minutes. We were directed down a cement hall. The walls were painted yellow, yet they did not appear bright at all. It was a dank and cold yellow that almost mocked us as we walked, shouting the hopelessness of so many that had walked that hall before us. It led to a small elevator that smelled like musty cigarettes and BO and took forever to move from one floor to the next. I could feel my insides shaking. Every part of me felt uncertain. The elevator doors opened slowly and we followed the hallway around to another smaller hall with tiny windows lined up on either side. We were directed to a window halfway down on the right. I can still see myself as I met his gaze, like an out of body experience. My legs went weak, panic began to rise up from my feet to my neck, I felt dizzy and disoriented. Suddenly a cry from deep within my soul forced its way out of my chest. It filled the air in the hallway, "My son! Oh my God, my son!" My husband, Brian, grabbed me to keep me from collapsing.

I am a pretty tough woman, but I was no match for the weight and intense pain of seeing my child there…through a 1 ft x1 ft square in a cement wall covered with bars. He begged me not to cry, said it looked bad for him, but it was beyond my control. Something else had taken over completely. I can't even remember what was said the rest of the time we were there. I just know that at that moment my heart was smashed into a billion pieces that to this day have not been completely restored.

At this point in my life, I had been in ministry for something like 18 years. I had seen some stuff. I had created some junk of my own, overcome some struggles, thought I had been through the worst of it all. I had even walked through some very hard times in my marriage and a period of questioning God's very existence…

while in ministry...but that's a whole different book. By this time my husband and I were pretty solid, God and I were good, life was moving along. This turn of events changed all of that. My life was seemingly derailed, nothing felt the same. I found myself in a cloud of depression, riddled with anxiety and gripped by fear. I had lost all control of my own emotions. I remember being unable to sleep, all I could do was lay there and run through the many scenarios of what might lie ahead. Out of desperation I found myself looking for something to put me to sleep. Over the previous summer we had guests who left some canned margarita drinks in our basement refrigerator. Without hesitation I grabbed one, along with a coloring book and colored pencils. While Brian slept in the bed next to me I drank away my fear and colored pictures that made me forget how ugly life was...but only for a moment. The next morning I had to wake up. I had to make myself get out of bed. I had to put on clothes and brush my teeth and pretend that I wasn't dying inside. I had to smile and love and do all the things that were so dang hard to do. And the day moved on like any other day. And I waited for the phone to ring so I could hear his voice on the other end and know that, for now, at least he was still alive.

Nighttime came again and brought with it the demons I had become too familiar with. They kept me from sleep and kept me from peace. So once again I reached into the fridge, once again I sat up and tried to color my life okay. This went on for as many days as I had drinks. Looking back I can only imagine what Brian must've thought when he woke up each morning that week. His wife passed out next to him with a coloring book on her chest and an empty can on her nightstand. I'm sure one drink a night is not really alarming to most. You might even be laughing at me for only needing one to go to sleep. But in my world it may as well have been poison. I grew up with an alcoholic parent and swiftly followed in her footsteps before I met Jesus. So I am certain my husband was talking to God more than ever that week.

Day 6 rolled around and I knew I had nothing in the fridge to help me sleep. I grabbed my keys to head for the store and God stopped me in my tracks. "No, Libbie, that's not for you." Don't panic, His voice wasn't audible, it never has been. It has always been in my heart, a nudge, a pull. This time, in fact, He took me directly to a Scripture in Proverbs 31:4:

It is not for kings, Lemuel—it is not for kings to drink wine, not for rulers to crave beer.

I'm not making a theological statement here. My husband has a beer now and then. I am simply saying that God, in His mercy, stopped me from going down a self-medicating path that would have destroyed my entire life. I stopped in my tracks and prayed. In my brokenness, I asked Him, "What else can I do, God?! I'm desperate!" His response? "Have you asked me to help you?" I hadn't. I had not prayed for help for myself at all. I had only prayed for Branden. But my soul was in trouble. And no doubt my husband and my younger children were as well. They were in the same story as me. Living the same nightmare as I. The only difference was the perspective. And to add to their concern I was totally losing it. That night I prayed when I climbed into bed. I asked God to help me rest. To give me peace. I remembered a Scripture about the Holy Spirit praying through us when we didn't know what to pray. So I prayed as I fell asleep. I began to rest again, in between court days. I could do normal daily life for the most part. But court days were hard. I remember the crushing experience of the first day of testimony.

As I sat in the courtroom I couldn't believe I was there, it was all just so surreal. I had to be dreaming, and I would wake up soon. This was not in my plan for his life, it was never a thought in my mind. Being there just felt wrong in every way. The wood paneling on the walls reminded me of a 70s crime show, the musty smell permeated from every corner of the room there was nothing warm and comforting about this place. the downright frigid

7

temperatures made it difficult to discern if my shaking was from the cold or from my fear of what was to come. I sat fidgeting, waiting, listening, watching. Young person after young person flashed up on the monitor or stood before the judge in person, charged with one crime after another. Most, if not all, were related to drugs.

In fact, that was why I was there that day. It was a fact, but it was still so hard to wrap my mind around. I am certain that no child ever dreams of becoming a drug addict when they grow up, and I certainly never had hopes of it for my son. No, he would be a veterinarian or a lawyer, or even a preacher. Surely he would not become a drug addict. How could he? I spoke Scripture over him the entire time he was in the womb. His birth was celebrated, as was every single accomplishment from that moment forward. He was loved and adored as a child who was very much wanted. Sure, there were mistakes made. I was far from a perfect parent. His father and I divorced when he was an infant. While I believed he was a Christian he lived a very different life in hiding. It was a life that would come out shortly after my son was born. If I had thought leaving wasn't the best thing I never would have done it. I remarried when he was 3 and my husband loved my son too. We raised him in a Christian home, attended church every week. I was a Worship Minister for goodness sake. Surely I would not have a son who would grow up to become an addict.

And yet there I sat. In a cold, damp courtroom, waiting to see my son ushered into the room in handcuffs and an orange jumpsuit. I wasn't so sure my heart could take it. No, I was actually sure that my heart could not. As I sat there I said in my head over and over again the Scripture God had brought to me when this battle first began. Proverbs 3:5, trust in the Lord with all your heart and lean not on your own understanding, in all your ways acknowledge Him and He will direct your paths. "Yes, I trust you God", I thought as I sat staring at the judge, "I trust you with his life."

The door opened and in he came; my handsome, sweet boy. His facial hair had grown in scruffy and he was disheveled. When I looked at him I saw the little boy he had once been, before he started down this dark path. I was unaware back then that he had chosen this. He told me recently that he had been just 12 years old when a friend at school offered him Marijuana. Despite everything we taught him, all he had been told, he said yes. It was the first step on a winding spiral to the depths of my deepest despair. He was someone completely different when he was on drugs. Someone I didn't know, and didn't want to know. The enemy had stolen my son from me. I was grieving the loss of every moment and my heart was devastated.

Testimony began. Every single word was like a dagger piercing my heart. Drugs, masks, guns...I knew these things coming in, but still, my heart was not prepared. He was facing 22 years in prison. 22 years. I was sure I was bleeding out right there in the courtroom. I was afraid to look down for fear I would see a puddle of blood beneath the bench I was seated on. Nausea began to swirl inside of me, I wasn't sure if I would pass out or throw up. I had to get a handle on myself. I forced myself to breathe and look around. I glanced down at the floor, no blood. My heart was still intact, but how? How was that possible? I could feel that it had been ripped right from my chest. But it wasn't, and no one noticed the complete devastation of a mother sitting in the midst of her worst nightmare. I was living the longest two hours of my life.

Finally, it was over. My son glanced my way and blew me a kiss. I sucked in what little air I could manage and kissed him back. My son. My precious son. How did we get here? There was guilt and shame, fear and frustration, anger and hopelessness. These feelings were all warring on the inside of me, fighting to take root and to destroy my soul. I stood up, numb from the experience. I'm not sure how my legs found their way out of the courtroom and to my car. Somehow I managed to fumble through my purse and find my keys. I fell into the driver's seat, closed the door behind me, and wailed. Sounds from deep within me filled the air, cries for mercy and the grace of a God I knew was real but that felt so far away in that moment. My son. My precious son.

I began to rifle through the files in my brain, through the Scriptures that had filled my prayers in recent days. "God, remind me what You said, remind me of Your promises, I believe they are real." I sat there, breathing in and out for what seemed like an eternity. Gradually I began to remember. I remembered the Scriptures God had led me to in my prayer time, when I cried out to him to rescue my son. He reminded me that this battle was not about this life. It was not about a boy who would grow into a man and have a career and live a life on this earth. No, it was about a soul. One single soul, and the fight for where it would one day reside. My fight was for his soul. So, in the car that afternoon, I lay my son down on the altar again. "Here he is, God. Save his soul by whatever means necessary." Yes, the hardest prayer I have ever prayed. If it took time in prison to rescue his soul, then so be it. I surrendered my own will in order to follow God's. Only He knows our future.

With trembling hands, I opened the Bible that sat on the seat of the car. I turned the pages that were worn and written on and came to Ezekiel 36:26. I prayed from this portion of Scripture the prayer I had prayed so many times lately. "God, give my son a new heart and put a new spirit in him. Remove his heart of stone and give him a heart of flesh. Put Your Spirit in him that he would be careful to keep your laws."

Why am I telling you this? Am I simply vomiting my painful memories to purge myself of the past? No. In the midst of a previous battle in my life, I made a promise to God. I told Him that nothing in my life would be wasted. He made the same promise to me. And He made that same promise to you. The Scripture says in Romans that all things work together for good for those who love the Lord and are called according to His purpose. So I will share these moments, these dark memories, in hopes of reaching you. In hopes of showing you that there is still hope. Even when hope seems gone. Yes, even when it feels like you are bleeding out in a courtroom full of oblivious passersby. There is hope. When you feel like you are too far gone, I promise you that you are not. Nothing is too difficult for Him. Whatever you are facing right now...it is not too difficult for Him.

Remember the book I tucked behind the driver's seat of my car? The one written by Carol Kent, about her imprisoned son. I took it out. It became my courtroom reading. It's amazing how much time is spent waiting in court. In the waiting and reading, I found I wasn't the only Christian parent, the only Minister, grappling with the shame of a child's choices. I learned that surely, someone else who loves Jesus has a child on drugs. Surely, someone else who loves Jesus has sat in a courtroom praying for their child. Someone else is hurting too. I am not alone. Someone else struggles with shame.

Shame seems to come up a lot in my life. It had become an old, unwanted friend of sorts. I mean, I brought shame into adulthood with me from my childhood. I had known it most of my life. But shame was delivered differently this time. It was present constantly. Every time someone asked how Branden was I faced shame. Most often I just said he was okay. That answer is completely appropriate, of course. It's not necessary for the entire world to know my business. But sometimes I knew I was supposed to talk about it, yet shame prevented the words from coming out. Every time I saw Branden's friends from school I felt shame at the contrast between his life and theirs. Shame came from all of the questions I was constantly asking myself. Had I done this to him? Was this because his father and I divorced when he was a baby? Or maybe it was our out of state move. Had I stayed and not allowed him to live with his father, maybe things would be different. Was I such a horrible parent that I made this happen? Shame came from the idea that if I were really a good Christian this would not have happened at all.

That idea had been planted somewhere in the early years of my faith. And it brought with it the shame of questioning, once again, if God was really good. If He was good surely this wouldn't be happening. Right? Come on, I know you've thought it. he knows you've thought it. And it's okay. These are the things that create "the working out of our salvation" talked about in Philippians 2. If we do not question how can we find the truth? Of course, I had to bring each of these thoughts to God and ask Him to sort through them with me. I had to sit in quiet before Him. I had to read His Word and seek out the answers. I had to cry and ask and pray. And He is a God of His Word. Seek and you will find, ask and you will receive, knock and the door will be opened. Maybe not today, maybe not tomorrow. Maybe that door has been nailed shut and it's gonna take some time to pull the nails of the lies of the enemy out and pry it open. Be patient, do not give up. Work out your salvation with fear and trembling and the light of day will break through the door again. You will know deep down inside that it is not your fault, difficult things happen because we live in a fallen world, God is still good and you do not have to wear shame like a Scarlet letter.

I find that God sends a beacon of hope often in the final moment, when we feel as though hope is drawing it's last breath. We can almost hear the count...three...two...then bam! That door of hope flies wide open.

CHAPTER TWO

I was worn out by the fight, disheartened by the challenges that seemed to continually arise. Branden's attitude was less than great the last time I had seen him. He was reading a Bible in jail, but still did not claim Jesus as his savior. He still considered himself a Buddhist. I struggled to understand how he could be so low and still refuse to see the truth. I was constantly fighting the fear that he would die before accepting Christ. The fear gripped my heart like a vice at times, immobilizing me in a state of panic. The charges filed against him were Federal in nature. His attorney was working on a defense and asked for his school papers to show that he could be a functional part of society. I was asked to locate a file cabinet that had been stored at a friends house. I remember how stopping there made me feel "icky". I know, it's such a ridiculous word, but it really is the best way to describe it. This addiction, the lifestyle he chose, found me in places I would never have gone. Ever. But a mother does not see danger for herself when her child's life is at stake. I had been to homes on streets long abandoned. I had been to motels and side streets because he had called to be picked up. I went, and would continue to go. Branden's friend opened the door in his underwear, smoke slowly snuck out between him and the door frame. I tried not to think about the way Branden had been living, in this house, with these friends. It was in stark contrast to my life, the lives of my other two children.

My mind cut to them. My babies. I wanted to protect them too. My heart hurt over how this situation had affected them. Amelia seemed to cut it all off. He was wrong and she would not allow his choices to affect her life. She hardened her heart toward him, and that worried me just as much as the pain it was causing me. And then there was Wyatt. He is ten years younger than Branden. His big brother was his hero. I remember the day I told them that Branden had been arrested. In Wyatt's innocence, he tried to find a simple explanation. Maybe the gun wasn't his. Maybe he was protecting himself from a bad guy. No, unfortunately not. Heart-wrenchingly not. Sorry, precious boy, your brother is the bad guy. I was angry that I had to look into his eyes and watch his heart break. His compassion for his brother has not waned, though, he still holds out hope. And I still find myself in places I don't want to be.

I was told to meet the friend in the garage. I walked around and he came to open the door. The file cabinet was there, in the midst of a bunch of other stuff. It was all strewn around. The garage was in complete disarray. He helped me put the file cabinet in my trunk and I drove away.

I pulled into a fast food parking lot, drove to the back and parked the car. I was waiting to pick up Amelia just down the street from there. I decided that while I waited I would sort through the stuff in the drawers. I began digging through the mounds of school papers and past due bills in search of his high school diploma and college transcripts when I saw it there. It was at the very bottom of the drawer, dusty and facedown. It was in a stately looking black frame, as if it were something of utmost importance. I turned it over and looked at it for a moment. I could not have imagined the emotions it would stir on the inside of me. My breath caught in my chest as my eyes scanned the document. His name was there in bold print, the font was so official looking. Beneath his name were the words, "Baptized into Christ". It was true, he had been, when he was 13. It seemed like a lifetime ago, like maybe it was someone else. The memory seemed yellow and jagged, the way my heart felt at that moment as it worked so hard to beat on the inside of me.

Surely this document couldn't belong to this same young man who now proclaimed Buddhism as the truth, this young man who threw everything away for the momentary pleasure and lifelong pain that drugs would bring. The young man whose words held no memory of the bond of love we had once shared. It couldn't have been his...but it was.

I looked at the name again, just to be sure. There it was, just as I had written it on his birth certificate, back when my dreams for him were as big as his potential. Back when I imagined I would sit in the crowd of smiling faces as he graduated from college to venture out on his chosen career. When I dreamed of the day I would see him receive his beautiful bride, and when I imagined the smell of my newborn grandchild in his arms. Those days were so distant, so painfully unattainable before me.

As I stared at the words, unable to put the dusty frame down, a thought began to form on the inside of me. At first, it was in slow motion, like it was trying to make its way through a thick layer of dark sticky tar. But then, as if it broke free from what held it back, it began to run quickly through my mind, over and over. It became a thought that began to breathe hope back into my lifeless heart.

Perhaps that certificate was there, in the bottom of that drawer, for a reason. Perhaps it was still framed and kept safe because it actually WAS a document of utmost importance. Wouldn't this be why it was found there, in the same safe spot as his diploma and college transcripts? It must have been just as important in his mind. Maybe not at the forefront of it, but at least somewhere in the distant recesses.

Truth be told, a man who had found true freedom in Buddha would not hang on to a piece of paper that tied him to Christ. It would have ended up in the trash, or at the very least lost along with the countless other unimportant items in his life. But no, not this. This was the thing that still proved who he once chose to be. A Christian, a child of the living God. The righteousness of God in Christ Jesus. It was a documented fact, one that he chose to be reminded of. And the Bible said that if I raise him up in the way he should go, when he is old he will not depart from it. He is not yet old. Not yet. As I looked the document over again, it didn't seem to be quite as yellowed. The dust didn't seem quite as thick.

I took a deep breath and thanked God for the reminder. The reminder that my son was also His son. The reminder that He doesn't forget and He doesn't give up. Therefore, neither could I. My trust had to be completely in Him to bring my son back to Him again. Branden was running full speed away from the only Hand that could save him, but that Hand was steady and patient. Once again, God showed Himself faithful to me that day. I knew He was still with me, still holding on to me.

He was always there, holding me, just like that day in the parking lot. His hand was so visible in it all. To me, to Branden, to any- one who was a part of the story. All the way back to the first day in court. That day, as I sat in the courtroom waiting for Bran- den's court-appointed attorney to arrive I watched and listened. Oh, yes, I said court-appointed attorney. And yes, that was a very difficult decision. My husband and I, along with Branden's father and his wife, prayed about what to do. We all agreed that we would not hire an attorney. See Branden is an addict. And addicts often find themselves in trouble over and over again. Their par- ents often spend everything they have to try to rescue them. To no avail. We believed God was saying 'watch and see what I will do'.

That day, as I watched, my stomach was in knots. I saw every court-appointed attorney act as though they did not care at all what happened to their clients. They were cold and disinter- ested. Almost all of them. All but one, that is. She was a small, older, attractive blonde. She had lovely blue eyes and was dressed to the nines. Her voice was soft, but she had a confidence about her. I heard her speak to her client and their family and compassion flowed from her heart. I sat there and prayed silently to my Father. "Lord, I know this won't be easy, I know Branden already has an attorney, but God I want her. Please, God, give us her." About a half hour later I heard the Bailiff call her over to the desk. "Endaluz' attorney can't make it, do you have time to take another case?" My heart stopped. I held my breath while I waited for her response. "Yeah, sure." And just like that God kicked down a door. Just like that my Father heard my cry and moved heaven and earth in response. My God. I cried. I sat there and cried at the realization that He was really right there with me. That He had not left me or forsaken me in that courtroom. He heard me and His mercy is real.

His mercy is real for you too. He has never left you, or forsaken you. I know you think you feel His absence at times. I do. I know you wonder how you could feel so much pain if He were really there. Open your eyes and look for Him. He is in the smallest things. He is in the biggest things. The Bible says that He knows every sparrow, he knows every hair on your head. Don't worry, you are far more important than a sparrow. And He loves you. He loves you so much that He sent His Son to take your place and pay the fee for your sin. I wish that meant there would be no pain in this life. I wish that meant no one in my family or yours would do drugs or go to jail. But it doesn't mean that at all. What it does mean is that whatever we face in this life, whatever trouble we find ourselves in, He will be there with us. We will not face this life alone. Ever. Psalm 139:7-10 says...

Where can I go from your Spirit? Where can I flee from your presence? If I go up to the heavens, you are there; if I make my bed in the depths, you are there. If I rise on the wings of the dawn, if I settle on the far side of the sea, even there your hand will guide me, your right hand will hold me fast.

17

You may feel like you are slipping, even falling out of control, but He will hold you fast if you cling to Him. He does, He will. You could run away and go live on an island on the far side of the sea and He will still be there! And he will use whoever he can to work in your life. Just like he used Branden's attorney.

He used her to work one miracle after another in Branden's case. Charges were dropped, considerations were made. Armed robbery changed to unarmed robbery. That was a HUGE deal. The attorney was thoughtful and caring. She worked very hard to get the two federal offenses Branden was charged with hidden on his record. This would mean that he could have a career and those offenses would never show up in a background check. He could honestly start over. Unfortunately, when young people are caught up in addiction and the lifestyle that comes with it they do not think about what their choices could mean for the rest of their lives. Branden had never given it a second thought. He never imagined that he may find himself applying for job after job only to be rejected because he carried with him a criminal history. He never imagined that the lack of a job could also mean trouble with supporting a family. He never imagined. But I did. I imagined it all. All the time. I held my breath more than I allowed my lungs to fill back then. Court day after court day I prayed and asked God for grace. 6 months in I thought it was finally going to be over. I thought I would never have to take the walk from my car to the courtroom again. It was finally sentencing day.

We watched God move mountains on Branden's behalf. We saw Branden's heart soften after being sober for 6 long months. But that morning would not play out as we had hoped. As soon as we arrived we were informed of a second case against Branden. This one was a year and a half old. Another felony charge, another trial. I did not think I could survive it. Really. At that moment, despite all God had done, I was certain I was through. Just count me in with the Israelites in the desert. I just couldn't do it anymore. I Should have been closing a painful chapter, but instead, I was facing an ongoing saga. The prosecutor decided Branden had been given enough breaks. These charges would stand. Possession with intent to deliver an illegal substance. We would have to wait four more weeks before any indication of what Branden's future would hold. The news was almost too much for him as well. He was crushed at the thought of what was ahead now. We all were. I gently touched his shoulder and spoke the words that I so desperately needed to hear at that moment. "God's timing is perfect, He is in control. So we wait and we trust."

We walked back into the courtroom, silent, broken again. And once again, my son pled guilty. I sat watching, listening with tears streaming down my face. Again, I knew the charges, but yet again my heart was not fully prepared. I wanted to stand up and scream This could not be real! I saw him there, looking so handsome in his blue suit. I imagined him at the podium at his college graduation. That's where he should be. Just 4 more classes. He was taking them when he was arrested. Almost done, almost there.

I took out a pen and wrote in the cover of my book the Scripture that had already been burned on my heart. I needed to see it with my eyes again. So I wrote Proverbs 3:5 I trust You Lord with all my heart. I do not lean on my own understanding. In all my ways I acknowledge You, direct my paths Lord.

In the car on the way home, the tears fell as I talked to my Savior, the One who holds the universe. I was telling Him that I do trust Him, even though I may not understand, I fully trust.

In that moment I thought about where Branden's heart was. I realized that the extensions, the months that kept getting added, they were Gods mercy. My son's heart was not fully surrendered, he was not in a place of humility yet. I knew it was true. Even with all that God had done he still did not trust Him. These 4 weeks were a clear gift of mercy for my son's heart. A merciful gift of one more chance, a merciful gift of opportunity to give it all to Him before the gavel falls once and for all. My heart was grateful. In the midst of the pain, there was gratitude for the mercy of the Father. I prayed for my son from a Scripture I had written out in Psalm 51, have mercy on my son, o Lord, according to Your unfailing love, according to your great compassion. Blot out his transgressions, wash away his iniquity and cleanse him from sin.

The days that followed were eerily slow, and yet dizzyingly fast. The final court date took forever to arrive, but had arrived in what seemed like only moments. The sound of my alarm that morning was not at all welcomed. The light from the windows made me close my eyes again. Somehow I slid out from under the covers and set my feet on the ground. I had to get ready for the day ahead. Could I? Could I possibly be ready for the day ahead? Probably not. The attempt would surely be futile. I tried nonetheless.

The reflection in the mirror was much older than the one that looked back at me at the start of the year. She did not yet know what was ahead of her. Her innocent smile held no sign of what was yet to come. She hadn't yet prayed the prayers of faith and desperation that would flow like rivers from her heart. She hadn't cried the many tears that would fall like heavy rains on thirsty ground. For sure, this day she was older. I turned away from her, trying to forget the lines on her face and focus on what was yet to take place.

I stepped into a suit with a robot-like motion. The zeal for life and joy that had once been typical of me was nowhere to be found. Plain black was all that was fitting for the day. I felt as though I needed to look as drab as the building I would walk into for one final hearing. I slipped my feet into a pair of black flats to prepare for the few blocks I would have to walk to get to the courthouse. It was time to learn his fate. I whispered quietly, "I trust You, Lord".

Images of the little boy he had been ran through my mind. I tried to push them aside so I could get ready without crying, but I couldn't. I could only see his innocent eyes and hear his sweet little voice calling me mommy. He was my love. I could question where I went wrong, but I've walked that road and it leads to a free fall of hopelessness and guilt. "Today I trust You, God."

When I arrived at the courthouse he was talking with his attorney, looking so handsome in his stately blue suit, his hair cut short and his face clean-shaven. My eyes did not want to look away for fear that I might not see him again. "I trust You, Lord."

A short time later we walked into the courtroom and we waited. We sat side by side thinking, hurting, praying. Waves of nausea began to sweep over me once again. I had prepared myself mentally before I came, I had done this before. But I learned that there is no way to prepare your heart to be smashed into a million pieces. It cannot be done. There is no preparation for the soul-crushing words spoken in a courtroom. I decided to flip through a magazine to distract my mind. I struggled to understand the words before me, my brain refused to focus. Then, right there in the pages of my intended distraction, God reminded me once again who He is. The writer of the article I was staring at shared a Scripture from Zephaniah 2:17:

> *The Lord your God is with you, the Mighty Warrior who saves. He will take great delight in you; in His love He will no longer rebuke you, but will rejoice over you with singing.*

He is a mighty warrior who saves. He is a Mighty Warrior Who Saves.

My thoughts began to calm my heart, "He saved my son on a cross long ago. He saved my son in a raid 8 months ago. He saved my son in a courtroom today. He saved my son. He is with me." Yes, right there in a loveless courtroom, He was with me. As I prayed to not fall apart in front of strangers, He was with me. As I watched them take my son away, He was with me. My heart was broken, but He was with me.

Where can I go from your Spirit? Where can I flee from your presence? If I go to the heavens, you are there, if I make my bed in the depths, you are there.

If I sit in a courtroom drowning in grief, You are there. If I cry unending tears alone in my car, You are there.

Now sitting in the parking lot, I waited for the tears to stop long enough to allow me to drive my numb body back home. I could hear the church bells ringing nearby, announcing the time. Their sound announced a new hour, a new position, a new start. It was time to leave the previous 8 months behind and move ahead stronger, filled with more faith than before, more confident in the God who never left me alone through it all. For certain I could now say, I trust You, God.

It's strange the things that are revealed in us in our times of trial and tragedy. What we believe is truth comes to the surface, whatever it is.

CHAPTER THREE

There is no doubt that it took a trial, a tragedy to develop my complete and utter trust in the Father. I had to find myself with nowhere else to go. And just because my faith grew immensely does not mean the story would end the way I wanted it to. That chapter ended well, all things considered. Branden was given only four months in jail...honestly a miracle. He had also been given 2 years of probation and a list of "dos and don'ts" I wish I could say the story ended there. I wish I could say he cleaned up. Only I cannot. He did not. And I continued to battle the thoughts that would try to take me down along with him.

Most often the thoughts were accusations rooted in truth. The Bible says the enemy is the accuser of the brethren. He isn't going to accuse us of things that won't sting. No, he will find the thing that we already struggle with. Yes, he will take truth and weave it tightly with his lies. He may even find some people to throw in their threads of painful words to really strengthen his cords of torment. He knew just what to point to with me. First, he pointed to my divorce from Branden's father; and second, he pointed to a move our family made when Branden was 16. My marriage had been in trouble and we were working hard to fix what was broken. We felt God leading us away from our hometown, somewhere we could focus on us. By that time Branden had been in much trouble. He had actually begun to run from us. As is common in many marriages, the struggles with a troubled teen were weighing heavy on our relationship. We prayed a move away would be good for Branden. But things didn't quite go the way we had hoped. Branden refused to go with us. In fact, he threatened to run away if we took him. He wanted to live with his father.

My ex-husband had given his life back to Christ and had always been involved in Branden's life. As difficult as it was for me, I knew his Dad was the only hope we had for getting him back on track. So we celebrated Branden's 16th birthday with a party before we left. I remember feeling like my body was being split in two as we drove away from Michigan, leaving him there. We stayed in Texas two and a half years, and I begged Branden to move there. He visited us several times, but to my dismay, he refused to stay. I missed him deep in my bones, it was a grief I didn't realize existed. A grief over someone who was still alive. I've become very familiar with that grief now. It resides deep inside of me somewhere and shows itself from time to time. My heart was bruised beyond recognition. Branden's struggles continued to escalate and he eventually ran away from his Dad. Shortly after that, we moved back to Michigan. One day, in a heated discussion, Branden's feelings flooded out at me. He told me I left him...that I had packed up and left him behind. As I looked at the pain on his face and his tears my heart froze. The pain was so intense I couldn't even take a breath. I threw my arms around him and cried. Over and over I said I was sorry. I told him how much I love him. When Branden left that day I was so steeped in guilt I could hardly stop crying. This was the moment the enemy took me back to over and over again. My son's perception was his reality. I had abandoned him. Despite the fact that I wanted nothing more than for him to come with us, I had abandoned him. Despite the fact that I did everything short of forcing him, I had abandoned him. We weigh the options and make our choices and pray we get it right. But in the end, we are only human. There's no way to foresee how the story will go. I had to remind myself what was true and what was confused in the mind of a troubled teenager. Should we have stayed in Michigan? Maybe. Would it have changed Branden's course? Probably not. Although I know I wanted Branden with me, I had to understand that he felt unwanted. He needed my apology. I gave it freely. And whether or not my actions played a role in Branden's choices, I have to make a choice of my own to bring my past to God and let Him use it. All of it, the good and the bad.

This is your choice too. You cannot let guilt keep you from being who God has created you to be. You cannot let the enemy control your thoughts, you have to be alert. Come to terms with the struggles of your past, and lay them down at the foot of the Cross and let them go. This doesn't mean you will never battle your thoughts again. It just means you have chosen to move beyond the struggle. It's not easy. Sometimes negative thoughts are obvious, we can see them coming. Sometimes they come like a sucker punch. Oh, how I have felt the sucker punch.

One time in particular, we had driven 16 hours over 2 days to get to our extended family. It was the week of my nephew's wedding. I had been so excited to get to the sunshine and to spend time with my family. How could I have known the words would hit me so hard? My sister and I stood in the kitchen over a steeping cup of tea and she shared a conversation she had with her husband. She simply posed the question to him, "Can you believe our son is getting married?" The words alone were innocent, even sweet... yet they assaulted my heart like an AK47. As soon as they were airborne the thoughts began bombarding my mind...

You will never stand with anyone in anticipation of your son's wedding.

You have failed as a parent.

You still have 2 more kids to raise to adulthood, YOU CAN'T DO IT.

I didn't even have a chance to form an argument. I was simply taken aback...then deflated as I tried to think of a response that would give me the strength to smile as the family celebrated. I managed to get through the rest of the evening and we made our way to our hotel. That night I was bombarded with reminders of every bad decision I had ever made. My future was questioned, my faith shaken. Over the next couple of days as I watched her four children laugh together, pose for pictures and talk about their bright futures my heart took on darker hues and a heavier feel as I thought of the time my son had spent in jail that year. I thought of the life he was continuing to live at that moment and I wanted to run far away from every reminder that I was the one who had failed. I didn't want to be forced to see the contrast. I just didn't think I could stand the pain. Then, of course, guilt began to set in. How could I be so self-absorbed at a time like this?! This was one of the most important days of my nephew's life! This was not about me!

It's amazing to me how the enemy can attack my mind with negative thoughts and then attack my mind for having negative thoughts. Yet, there I was once again trying to block the blows as they swung my way.

For the next couple of days, I felt as though there was a boulder on top of me, squashing every breath of air I could take. I knew I had to get out from underneath it and find life and breath again.

It happened when I reminded myself of a simple decision I had made previously. Remember? I decided that if I was to face such ugliness in life I would use it to somehow bring God glory. I know there are people out there who struggle with these same thoughts, with shame and regret. If I can use my experiences as encouragement to them that God can and will still use them, I will. And it will point to Him and proclaim His grace, mercy and unrelenting love.

And then I win. Yes, I win the fight with the enemy, and the boulder that threatened to crush me will become a platform for sharing the good news of the greatest love of all. I have to remind myself both where I have been, and whose I am, despite the contrast between the two.

This is a decision that you, too, must make. Will you try to tuck away your experiences? Or will you choose to stand believing that His ways are higher and His plans are good? Will you stand and use your struggles to reach into the hearts and lives of those around you?

God used this season in this story to teach me so much about myself, my heart and the changes that I still needed to make. And in the midst of it all, He allowed me to pray with woman after woman and speak life into their failing hearts. As I stood at the back of the church on Sunday mornings they would come. Women whose husbands had walked away from years of marriage to take the hand of someone else. Women whose children were addicted and spiraling out of control. Women who were alone and felt there was no future for them. One by one He brought them, one by one I prayed. Some days as I poured over the Word of God, He would highlight a Scripture for one of them and I would send it to them. Every time they would respond with gratitude and hope. God is good. His miracles are active. He wants to use you to show Himself to the people around you. Will you let Him? Nothing wasted. Nothing useless. Not even your mistakes. Will you let Him be your purpose? Will you let Him change you along the way?

I don't think I've ever really looked for lives to touch. I've just kind of been open to it. My dear friend has a son who has been in and out of trouble. He has struggled with drugs and alcohol, and even considered suicide. I've had a connection with this kid since he was very young. He's musically brilliant and has a voice that reaches down into the depths of the soul. When he was 19 he was at a crossroads in his life, about to walk away from God and chase after the world. He had no idea that what the world offered was a counterfeit. He just knew that he was hurting and needed to find a remedy. It just so happened that we needed a musician for our youth band for summer camp, so I asked him to join us. It was one of those things you can look at and know that God was orches-trating. Our youth worship leader and him became good friends and I watched God reach into his life and save him. My eyes well up with tears just recalling what God did. When our youth worship leader left for college this kid stepped in and led the band. He also began to lead adult worship with me. I watched God grow him and lead him. Not that there weren't bumps in the road, there were. But there was also grace and mercy...and a better understanding of the love that we are called to.

One Sunday morning we showed his testimony on video during service. To that point, I hadn't known just how close to the edge he had been. He recounted a time in his car in the college parking lot when he downed a 5th and snorted some lines before class, and how he later drove his car to the river prepared to drive it in and end his life. I didn't know the depth of his torment that summer when we went to camp. But God did. He used a little camp and a bunch of teenagers to rescue His child. He is so very, very good. As I watched Logan's testimony I was filled with a mix of emotions. I was grateful that God had rescued him, amazed at what had been happening behind the scenes as I obliviously took him to camp with us. But I was also hurt. Hurt that it wasn't my son in the video. Angry that he was still out there living his life in opposition to what God planned for him. I sat in silence as the video played and inside I asked God why. Why not my son? "I could be watching his story, why am I not?" And in all His kindness God reminded me that what He did for Logan he will do for Branden too. He is no respecter of persons. He loves Branden as much as He loves Logan. Branden's rescue may not look the same, but I needed to hold out hope that it was coming. And the irony of having a son who was lost and being used to rescue someone else's son...well that's just how God works. We get to sow into the lives of others before we get to reap our own harvest.

And we don't always know God is working when we are in the middle of it. Just before the summer camp I had invited Logan to...just before God reached down and pulled Logan from the pits...I had written this blog:

Serving God has been one of the greatest joys of my life, and also the biggest challenge. It feels like a constant battle. Sometimes the people I am serving are the very people who leave the scars. Sometimes.

And sometimes all of the hard work is met with a lackadaisical attitude by those around and it feels easier to just walk away. So much easier.

Recently I was planning worship for a small Sr. High summer camp. Every time I thought I had it all nailed down, even to the point of practices going great, it all fell apart. One team member after another stepped out for various reasons. In my frustration I was chatting with a friend who shared this thought, "Just back out, it's just a little camp!" and in that moment I really wanted to. I really, really wanted to.

Not because I'm not excited about serving there, but because I'm tired of trying so hard to make it all work out.

A short time after that conversation I was talking to God in the car. I told Him that I know He is going to work this all out for good. I reminded Him and myself that I trust Him with all my heart, and I need for Him to guide my steps. I was lamenting a little, for sure... and then it happened.

An old familiar fire rose up in me...a new found commitment to the "little things". Perhaps being in a fast-growing church (that was larger when I jumped on board than most churches ever get) has skewed my view of things. I began to realize once again that any opportunity to minister is worth it. Even just one person...one teenager, one woman...any life that can be touched for His glory is worth any amount of blood, sweat and tears. Every heart-wrenching conversation...every hour of preparation for a seemingly too-small group...every prayer said, song sung, Word given, tear cried... all more than worth it.

All more than worth it.

As I sat down this morning to pray, not intending to write this, I was reminded of a Scripture.

Luke 16:10 whoever can be trusted with very little can also be trusted with much, and whoever is dishonest with very little will also be dishonest with much.

I know this is talking about money and property…but the principal is the same. How could I be trusted with bigger things if I cannot be trusted with this little camp? If I don't find the souls of these kids to be important, how can I be trusted to serve?

I'm not saying I will ever be used in much larger situations…please don't misunderstand.

I'm simply saying that every single soul…every single heart… every single teenage face that stands before me is vitally important to God. Therefore, it should be vitally important to me.

Whatever worship looks like at this camp, I will give it my all. I will approach it with prayer and hard work and ask God to work in it all…all the while remembering He said:

Therefore, go and make disciples of all nations, baptizing them in the name of the Father and of the Son and of the Holy Spirit, and teaching them to obey everything I have commanded you. And surely I am with you always, to the very end of the age. Matthew 2:19-20

What if I had listened to my friend that day and decided to just not go to camp? What if I had called the camp administrator and said, "Sorry, we just can't seem to get it together this year." Where would Logan be? Would he have encountered God that summer? Would he have ended up at our church leading worship and serving God? Or would he have found himself back in the school parking lot that fall with a bottle in his pocket and some powder on the dash? I don't know. But I do know that I'm glad I didn't quit. I'm glad I pushed through the hard stuff. In the midst of my own pain and hurt, I'm glad I pushed through the hard stuff.

I made a decision that if the enemy was going to hit below the belt and take my child, I would do the same and snatch as many others from the pits of hell as I possibly can. Each life is a seed, each prayer for them is a prayer for Branden. I'm watching for that first blade to pop up from the ground. For the hope of spring and new life. It's coming.

I used to think tragedies came one at a time, but with age, I learned that tragedy doesn't do math. It just shows up.

CHAPTER FOUR

In the midst of trying to steady my heart through all of the drama with Branden, I found myself writing my mother's eulogy. Not my idea of fun. I loved her. My greatest sadness at her death was honestly what we did not have together. Alcoholism stole her from me for the better part of my life, for the better part of hers too.

As I searched for the best words to describe the best parts of her I began to realize that in her leaving this life and entering the next, I was closer to stepping into what God has called me to. I don't really know how to pinpoint it, how to verbalize the sense that rose up inside of me. I just know that there were things she was called to do that she never did...there were lives she was called to impact that someone else had to. The disease that stole her from me also stole her from the world around her...from the purpose God had for her life. That truth has only solidified in me the drive to become what God has called me to be...to do what He has called me to do. Nothing wasted. All that has happened in my life both good and bad, all I have done, used for His glory. The enemy will not win.

One of the biggest truths about my mother's life is that she was strong. She would not go down without a fight. No way. She wasn't ready to die, and by golly, she wasn't going to until she said so. That fight is alive in me as well, I won't go down without a fight either. In fact, I won't go down at all. I mean I might hit the mat, but much like my mom, there will be no count of three. And on my way back to my feet I'm grabbing the hand of anyone nearby and pulling them up with me. A shot to the eye of the enemy every time. Just when he thinks one is down two come up... or three...or ten. Nothing wasted in my life. My mother gave me a determination that what was stolen from her will be multiplied in me. What the enemy meant for evil God has used for good. That's just how He is. It's just what He does. My mother was strong, because of her I will be stronger. Nothing wasted Lord, use every moment, every breath, every story, every tear. Use them to rescue, use them to reach and save. I'll go out guns blazing with my wagon full of souls.

I think my own background, my own childhood with an addicted parent, allows me to understand that Branden has a choice for his life. I think it might be what keeps me from taking on the blame and allowing shame to rule. Not that it's not a struggle. Sometimes I still have to fight my own bitterness over my childhood. Losing my Mother sent me into some dark thoughts and deep pain.

On this particular day I was having a childlike moment...not the good kind...where everything seems like green grass and sunshine. No, more like a tantrum, where in my head I was yelling "it's not fair!". It's not fair that they lived their story and I have lived mine. It's not fair, God. I sat alone in the car with tears streaming down my face. It's not fair. In His gentle, loving, correcting way he spoke to my heart. In order to live out your calling, you had to live your life. Silence fell hard on my heart. I didn't want to hear it, yet I knew it was true. Then again, words boomed into my heart, a question burned through the silence. "Would you want to give up what I called you to in order to have had their life?" Would I? It felt like a moment from It's A Wonderful Life. I honestly didn't even hesitate before I spoke, "No, Lord, I don't want anything else." It was true. But how? Why would I choose the pain of rejection, the failure? Why would I take that painfully broken path over the one that seems so much easier? Because I know that there is beauty in this brokenness. There is freedom in the surrender. There is a joy that can only come from watching Him use my past to alter someone else's future. I know that the path I walked leads to this spot right here. So I would say no to the easier path every time. Although I am not the sum of my struggles, those struggles have given me a heart for others who hurt. I can pray with a clear understanding and humility I would not have found any other way. My past has led me to this present, which is leading me to the future He has laid out for me. Loss only allows us to see what we have gained in a brighter light.

I hope I am not misleading you. None of what I am saying is easy. There are days I want to crawl into a cave and stay there. But each day builds on the next to grow our faith...and our faith is a strange sort of thing.

Sometimes we feel it, and sometimes our faith is a choice...a very hard choice. Sometimes we look into the face of an ugly, painful and unfair reality and it hurts. At that moment we have to choose. Is He still God? Is He still healer? Is He still life-giver?

I've stood on the edge of that choice more than once. I've gazed into the possibility of two very different realities. Every time His Love has won. Much like David I've spoken the words..."but God"...and they've refreshed my weary soul.

In Psalm 3, David is a broken man as his son is seeking to take his life. He has been through trial after trial and faced many failures. His heart is broken as he tells God that people are after him. But...in verse 3 he says, "but You, O Lord are a shield for me, my glory and the lifter of my head".

I'm pretty sure David wasn't feeling lifted at that moment, but he knew enough to speak truth from his mouth in the time of adversity. This is why he said in verse 5, "I lay down and slept, I awakened again, for the Lord sustained me." He was recounting to himself the goodness of God...a reminder to steady his heart. If you recall he did the same thing years before when he fought Goliath. He reminded himself of his prior victories before he attempted to take Goliath's head.

Sometimes all you can recall is that He put breath in your lungs today, that He woke you up this morning. That's a start. As you speak of God's goodness your heart will remember. Courage will rise up. Gratitude for what He has done will outweigh the pain as it did for David. And like David, you will say, "salvation belongs to the Lord".

It's not "positive thinking". It's a spiritual battle, most of which takes place in our head. The pain is real. The fallout is heartbreaking. But our hope is not in this world. Stand your ground when it's hard, speak the truth to yourself when you're not sure you believe. Keep your eyes fixed on the One who will dry every tear from your eyes.

Salvation belongs to the Lord and joy comes in the morning.

Those times of struggle will not last. There are times of trial and tragedy and times of joy. For everything, there is a season. Sometimes we have to purposefully step into the next season even when the weather hasn't changed.

I had not seen a change in the "weather" of Branden's situation. After being released from jail his life spiraled downward again. Any hope that he had permanently turned from drugs was a distant memory. I needed to forget that reality for a minute. So, we planned a family vacation. It was a much-needed vacation. On top of the weight of Branden on my heart, the summer was filled with youth camps and events that simply wore me out. Those were followed up by the loss of my mother and a couple of trips surrounding that. I was done. I wanted to spend time with my family, but the thought of another airplane, another long day of travel, was just overwhelming.

Yet, my kids were ecstatic at the thought of heading to Universal. So I packed a suitcase and a smile and headed out the door. A break from everything I had been living through was welcomed.

Three days into the trip we had a rest day. A day of simply laying around in a cabana by the pool and doing nothing. I napped and read and listened to podcasts. It was refreshing. One particular podcast discussed the idea that nothing in our lives is by chance. The preacher shared a story of being on vacation and experiencing a divine appointment. My heart felt a little jealous, I'm not gonna lie.

So I prayed, "Lord, thank You for this time with my family to have fun and rest. But I want you to use me here Lord. Somehow use me on this trip to touch someone's life". We went about our business and enjoyed our time together...and then we came to our last night of the trip.

We went out for dinner to the local Margaritaville. We sat outside and the place was hopping. It was noisy and jam-packed, and we were hungry. Our waiter approached the table with a smile and noticed my husbands Detroit shirt...his clothes start conversations everywhere we go.

In all honesty, I knew this was a God meeting from the moment he began talking. He told of his struggle over whether or not to return home to Detroit, the prayers of his born-again Mom, and his own agnosticism. I could clearly see God pulling at his heart. Before we left that night he had squatted down next to our table in this big, loud, busy restaurant and bowed his head. We prayed for God to smash into his life and show Himself to him in the quiet of the night. With our email addresses in hand and tears in his eyes, he hugged me as we went on our way.

My kids were amazed. I was elated. But that was not the end.

A few days later, back at home, God reminded me to pray for him. So as I drove around town I began to lift him up, which led me to thank God for his praying mom. The mom who looked her sons agnosticism in the face every day and said, "You don't win". The mom who cried out for a child her heart longed to have close, a mom who refused to give up.

And suddenly I saw her. I saw the reflection of my own face. This mom, right here, who at times feels there is no hope for my own child. I caught a glimpse into my son's world, where God sends strangers in response to my prayers, and my hope was restored in a moment.

So much came out of a simple prayer for God to use me...for a waiter in a town far away, for a mom waiting for her son to come home, for a family growing in our faith, for a mother's heart that needed hope. God is good, and nothing is ever by chance.

Psalm 37:23 The Lord directs the steps of the godly, He delights in every detail of their lives. NLT

These are the redeeming moments. There is joy in the midst of pain. There's good in the middle of the bad. We just have to open our eyes to see it. Open your eyes. Right now, open them. Where is God blessing you? Small or big. Where is He making Himself known to you? In the few years between Branden's first arrest and now I have experienced more laughter than any other time period in my life. It's true. Oddly enough, the summer before this all began I felt led to start homeschooling Amelia and Wyatt. I felt completely unqualified to do so, but I also felt led. I honestly do not believe that was a coincidence. I am convinced it was all God's perfect timing. In those two years, I discovered a deeper joy in parenting...a deeper closeness to my children. And I learned just how funny they are! Laughter became a healing balm applied to my broken heart by the joy of my children.

I know this sounds crazy, but they would record me having laughing fits in the car or at home. I have a pretty boisterous laugh and when others hear it they can't help but laugh as well. So they would record me and send it to their friends. I told them I want them to record me every time I laugh that hard. The plan is that all of those little video clips of me laughing will one day be cut together and played at my funeral. Yup, my funeral will be a laugh fest, you won't want to miss it. Why? Because laughter is good medicine. It's an honest-to-goodness gift from God. It has become a sort of thermometer that helps me check how I'm doing. When grief comes in and I feel heavy I make myself aware of whether or not I've laughed that day. If I haven't I let my family know, "We need to laugh!" and they never fail to make it happen. I am so grateful I figured this out, because life was not going to get easier any time soon. This story had not yet concluded.

It seemed as though any phone call from Branden's number would bring more heartbreak, more pain. My phone rang late one evening. He was crying on the other end. He said he just didn't think could bear the burden anymore. My voice stayed calm, but my heart was beating at double time. Where was he? Did he have a gun? Dear Lord, please tell me he didn't have a gun. "Who are you with, Branden?" I didn't want to cause him to hang up, but I had to figure out where he was. He was with his girlfriend, I asked him to put her on the phone and he did. "Where are you?" I asked as calmly as I possibly could. She obliged and told me. "Do not leave him alone, I'm on my way." As I spoke to her I motioned to my husband to grab his keys. He followed me out of the house to the car. The whole time I kept Branden on the phone with me. I just let him talk. He assured me he was not going to hurt himself. He was just tired. Tired of the effort it took to live the life he was living. When I told him I was pulling into the lot of the motel he panicked. "Don't come in Ma!" He always called me Ma. I really don't even know where he got it from. But it's what he calls me, and anytime I hear the word there is a mix of nostalgia and pain. "I'll come out", he said. It was freezing outside. The parking lot was covered in slick piles of ice. I saw him walking toward the car, the lights of the motel behind him. I opened the door and stepped out of the car. I remember the sound of the cars from the freeway and the smell of fast food in the air. I held him there, in the cold. He sobbed. His body shook as he let out years of pain and anguish. I could feel his bones in my arms. Just bones. Life had been hard. He was tired. And at that moment I was sorry for every thought I had ever had that was even remotely judgemental toward the parent of an addicted child. Because you don't really know pain until you've held your child's shaking body in the freezing parking lot of a drug infested motel. No, you can't possibly know.

He decided to let me go into the room. My step Mom pulled into the parking lot just as we were getting ready to go in. She has always been an amazing Grandma to my children. She is a therapist, and has counseled many a young person in similar situations. We all went inside and she began to do what she is so good at doing. Branden's girlfriend sat on the bed while Branden positioned himself on the edge, across from Grandma. Eventually, Grandma got around to a very important question. She said, "Do you have any drugs in the room with you?". "Just my prescriptions", the girlfriend replied. "Let me have them, I'll bring them back in the morning." See, this generation does drugs differently. They take what is legal and mix it, and abuse it to create a street-level high. It's deadly, really. As soon as the words hit the air Branden began to panic at the thought of not having access to those drugs. He was up and pacing, angrily, raising his voice. I saw my husband by the door, his hand on his side. I knew what was under his hand. He always carried, he worked in Detroit. He was a cool-headed man. I knew he would never act rashly, but I couldn't keep the fear of what could happen at bay. "Oh Lord, please, no." I was pleading with God to get control over the situation, to just calm Branden down. He had been a loose cannon for years, totally unpredictable. In what seemed like the longest moment of my life Grandma managed to calm him down, and get him to agree to let her take the drugs home with her." I saw his girlfriend on the bed, tears in her eyes. My heart froze in my chest. She had been first to agree to let us take those drugs, and Branden was angry over it. I sat down next to her while Branden was distracted. "Are you safe?" I asked. She shook her head yes. "Really? I can't leave here until I know you feel safe. I will help you." My voice shook as I spoke. "He would never hurt me", her response was firm. I nodded and stood up to leave, trying to wrap my brain around the fact that I had just had that conversation. Realization was setting in that my son was truly someone I did not know. The drive home was silent. The tears streamed down my face with no sound. There was no wailing this time, no audible sobs. Just silent tears. I don't know what was worse.

 "You know how to use a sword better than most. So pick it up and fight. You do battle!" My friend's words were like a beacon in the midst of a dense fog that was clouding my ability to determine a correct course. Before I called her my breaths were short and quick, my hands were shaking, and my stomach felt sick. I hadn't fully recovered from the heartache of having my niece checked into a psychiatric hospital the night before when Branden called again. This time from jail. Obviously, the call was not completely unexpected. It was actually more welcomed than the call I feared would come on his behalf. He was, at least, alive.

It's crazy how I can be sprinting through life, launching a church, meeting with friends to pray, having family days downtown...and suddenly a leg sweep comes and I find myself flat on my back. This time, honestly, the wind was knocked out of me. After the incident at the motel, Branden had to go before a judge again and he was going to go to rehab. We were just one day away. One day. I had tried for years to get him to go. Finally, the legal system was forcing him. Hope had been revived. And with a single phone call, it was snuffed out once again. Every cell in my body was screaming out in frustration and defeat.

I managed to put the credit card number into the phone so I could accept the call from my son. The voice on the other end confirmed my fear. He was frantic over the situation he had gotten himself into...again. Do we leave him there? Do we extend a hand? My husband and I prayed and struggled over what to do next.

It was a last-ditch effort. A Hail Mary. If we could just get him to rehab things might change. If he could see the world through sober eyes again he might see things differently. So we paid the cost, we drove the hours, only to have him run again. Hope dashed. Fear realized.

But by then, the sword had been drawn. By then my friend had already reminded me of whose I am. So the "run" didn't knock me out completely. The sword felt heavy and awkward in my weak hands. But it was there nonetheless. And the more I tried to lift it the stronger I got.

"I trust You, Lord, with all my heart", one weak swing of the sword.

"There's nothing too difficult for You", another swing, this one stronger.

"I run this race to receive a crown! I'm not going down before it's over!" The sword now in full swing.

For I am convinced that nothing will separate my son from the love of Christ. There is nowhere he can go that God is not present. My Lord leaves the 99 to chase after the 1. Today my son is the 1. Very soon he will be counted among the 99. My God does not relent. He does not relent so I will not lose hope. His hope is alive in me. He is good. He is God.

This is how I fight my battles.

This is how I fight my battles...

With a reminder from the friends God has placed in my life.

With the Word that is truth and life.

With the hope that is found only in Him.

This is how I fight.

Are you catching on yet? My hope here is that you will learn from my story how to fight through your own struggles and unbelief. My hope is that when you face what seems unbearable the words in this book will say to you, "You know how to do battle." Then you will pick up your sword, the Word of God, and begin to speak it out of your mouth. My hope is that every swing will breathe strength and life back into your weary body. My hope is that every trial will bring a greater determination to use what you have been through for the ultimate glory of God. My hope is that your words, your reach, will one day be used to save many, many souls. Nothing wasted.

Time went on and by now Branden was basically on the run. The judge said he had to go to rehab, and he didn't. It was just a matter of time until he would be picked up by the police. He couldn't just walk away from what he had done or what he had failed to do. He reached out to me less and less, and I had decided to stop chasing him. I prayed all the time. When he did call or show up, I received him with love. But, he was going to have to figure this thing out on his own. I couldn't save him. Eventually, he stopped calling altogether. I had moments where I imagined the worse. I don't know what was harder, knowing what he was doing or knowing nothing at all. I am sure some people judged me for my choices. It's easy to say you would chase your child down and force them to get help. The truth is that no one knows what they would do until in that situation. Remember that when you want to judge the choices of another parent. Be merciful. It could be you.

"You may have to fight a battle more than once to win it." Lisa Bevere, Without Rival

CHAPTER FIVE

The long silence was broken by my own inquiry. A text came through while I was teaching a class at our homeschool co op. This time it wasn't devastation I felt, it wasn't even sadness. No, this emotion was one that should have struck fear in the heart of my enemy. I was angry. With righteous indignation, I was angry. Angry that I was looking at what I was looking at. It was a screenshot from a friend who is a police officer. I had asked him to check on Branden for me. He sent a new list of charges, these were just a month old. Same old story, same old problems. But new emotions. How could he be so stupid? How could he throw away his opportunity for a second chance? How could he spit on the grace and mercy of God? And how could the enemy continue to win? How could his lies still be seen as truth? I was mad. Fighting mad. But my swings were not directed at my son....even though I was definitely mad at him. No, these swings were very calculated, very intentional.

> *Therefore I do not run like someone running aimlessly; I do not fight like a boxer beating the air. No, I strike a blow to my body and make it my slave so that after I have preached to others, I myself will not be disqualified for the prize.*
>
> *1 Corinthians 9:26-27 NIV*

I will not be taken down by this. I will not be weakened by the enemy's blows. I am well aware of who my enemy is.

> *For our struggle is not against flesh and blood, but against the rulers, against the authorities, against the powers of this dark world and against the spiritual forces of evil in the heavenly*

realms.

Ephesians 6:12 NIV

Right now, here today, I am taking swings. Every time I think about what my enemy has done to my child I take a swing. A very deliberate, very precise swing.

I have raised this child in the way he should go and when he is old he will not depart from it. (Prov 22:6) God will use this situation, it will, in fact, work together with the rest of the story for my good, for Branden's good, for God's glory. (Romans 8:28)

I trust You Lord with all my heart, with all my life. (Prov 3:5) This is not over. And I know how the story ends. My enemy will be thrown into the lake of fire for all eternity, the door locked and the key thrown away. (Rev 20:10) I will be in heaven with my Father forever. What can anyone do to me? Nothing. Because nothing can separate me from the love of God. (Rom 8:39)

Do you hear it? Can you hear the sound of my blows hitting the target? I can. I do. And with every blow, he gets weaker and I get stronger. This is how I fight. This is how we fight. Word by Word, swing by swing. The trials come ...the thoughts come, the Word... like a sword shoots from our mouth. Like a two-edged sword dividing between what is truth and what is a lie. What is truth? Whatever God says in His Word. What is a lie? Whatever the enemy whispers to you.

Use your weapon. Don't leave it there, unattended, unprepared. Why read the Word? Why own a weapon if you are not going to use it? Swing! Swing now! Swing fast! Swing hard! You will get better at it! You will become more precise. But by all means start swinging. Because he is winning - so start swinging. Because our kids are going down - so start swinging, because our marriages are failing - so start swinging. Right here, right now. SWING!

"In order that Satan might not outwit us, for we are not unaware of his schemes" (2 Corinthians 2:11) SWING! Do not be afraid. Look at the example of so many in the Bible. In the face of fear, they chose to be courageous and do what God was calling them to. You can do that too!

The story of Esther is just one example. It is so fascinating. If you haven't read it yet, put this book down and go read it.

So often this story is presented in a childish form. Almost like a fairy tale, like Cinderella. But please understand, Esther's story was no fairy tale. Esther was a Jew. Many Jews had been taken as slaves in Persia, which was where Esther was living. While her people had been freed to return to their homeland, many found it better to live in exile in Persia than to go back to a war-torn Jerusalem. To make matters worse in Esther's life, both of her parents died when she was a child. Her uncle raised her.

She didn't really have a bright future ahead of her. The king of the nation Esther's people served was not a man of God by any means. After a spat with the queen, he divorced her and decided to find a new queen. So he ordered that all the young women be brought in to be considered as a candidate for the queen. This is the part we tend to "clean up" like Esther was in some sort of beauty pageant. The ugly truth is that Esther was once again being sold…given over against her will to a veritable stranger. The story has so many incredible points and there's really so much to be considered. God moved in the worst of circumstances. Esther listened to wisdom and sought God by fasting and praying. She was destined for a life of poverty and obscurity, but God had different plans. Plans that included her being responsible for saving His people. And that is all true and it is all so good. But after leading a study on Esther I kept thinking about the word victim. I know it's strange, but God had been showing me that I had lived my life with an underlying belief that I was a victim, and that because of that I could not really fulfill God's plan for me.

It was a shocking revelation for me really because I see myself as quite strong. And honestly, the victim mentality annoys me. I'm more of a "get over it" kind of person. But...as I began to look deeper I saw that God really was pointing this out. He was asking me to deal with this thing on the inside of me that had kept me unknowingly imprisoned.

I had just started writing this book. But honestly, I wasn't entirely sure it was even a book. I was just sort of writing. I had a sense for a long time that God wanted to use me in a new way, a different way. Honestly, I felt like He was showing me that the reason I had not begun moving in the direction of His plan was because of me. He was there, just waiting for me to figure it out.

I picked up a book that had been on my nightstand for ten months. Yes, ten months. I always have a pile of books I'm working my way through and I hadn't gotten to it yet. I began to read Kill the Spider by Carlos Whittaker and it became abundantly clear that the timing was no accident. Seriously, if you haven't read this book, stop, again, and order it right now. It will change your life. The book basically said that there are things way deep down inside, lies from the enemy that we believe, and that they affect how we live our lives. I kept thinking of the ones I had known about for years...fear and shame. But I knew there was something else. Something I had no idea existed. A friend sent a link to a teaching by the author of the book and I watched it while I worked out one morning. He never said the word victim. It wasn't even a topic in his talk. But I heard it in my spirit loud and clear.

Later in my car, I asked God, "Is this for real? Do I really see myself this way? Help me understand." And I began to remember situations, reactions, ideas that had permeated my life. And I realized that I had, indeed, believed I was a victim. I didn't have a victim mentality, but I believed that everything that happened in my life was beyond my control and that it had all been unfair.

It's true, there are many unfair things that happened in my life, as both an adult and a child. Somehow I took those on as my identity. And I believed that because I had been damaged goods (so to speak), I would never be good enough for God. So I continually stopped myself from achieving because I didn't believe I could do anything good. I didn't believe I was good.

I had been praying for a couple of weeks about this lie I had believed, asking God how to deal with it. I had been writing out Scriptures that related. Then, when I taught about Esther, I saw her differently than I had before. I saw the choice she made to not allow her circumstances to shape who she would become. She was an orphaned slave with no future, offered up to a man she didn't know and then kept with all of his other trophy wives...no freedom, no hope for that to change. If anyone could have pitied herself for being a victim it was Esther. But she chose not to. She chose to believe the truth and not allow the lie to thwart the course of her life. The result was joy and blessing beyond measure...for her and all of the Jews in Persia.

God will move in the ugliest of situations. He will use the very thing that is oppressing you as the catalyst to set you free. He will speak to those around you, move on the hearts of people and change you. Yes, you. Our circumstances may not change, but if we stay close to God something even better happens...we change. And that changes everything.

Please don't misunderstand me. I am not, by any means, saying that you should stay in abusive situations. If that is your reality right now you need to find courage enough to leave. Seek help and get somewhere safe. And in the midst of that horrible situation, God will move.

The enemy would have you believe that you are damaged goods, unusable by God, unlovely to those around you. Yes, the enemy of your soul would leave you in obscurity for the rest of your life so you cannot be seen by anyone. In order to save the nation of

47

Israel Esther had to be seen. You have to be seen, by one or by one million. Whichever it is, you have to come out from the shadows of the lies you've believed and let your light shine. Your story is a part of that. Let Him use it to rescue His people. I know this is hard to believe. It is hard to really take on as truth. Even in unbelief, God can move.

If you are a reader, you've probably re-read books. And if you've re-read books, you've probably found that you see things the second time around that you didn't see the first time. The Bible is the same way. I've read it countless times, but there's always something new that jumps out at me. I was reading Romans 4 and saw something that made me pause. Look at this:

> *Against all hope, Abraham in hope believed and so became the father of many nations, just as it had been said to him, "So shall your offspring be." Without weakening in his faith, he faced the fact that his body was as good as dead—since he was about a hundred years old—and that Sarah's womb was also dead. Yet he did not waver THROUGH unbelief regarding the promise of God, but was strengthened in his faith and gave glory to God, This is why "it was credited to him as righteousness." (Romans 4:18-20, 22 NIV)*

Do you see the word I capitalized? Through. In other versions, the word "in" is used. But the word through stopped me in my tracks. How could he have maintained his faith THROUGH unbelief? I looked the word up. Check it out:

Through: 1) Moving in one side and out the other 2) Continuing in time toward completion.

So Abraham stepped in one side of unbelief and came out the other side by continuing to move in the direction God had pointed him, toward completion.

I mean, he obviously struggled with doubt at times, otherwise he wouldn't have tried his wife's idea of making a child with Hagar. Am I right? There had to be doubt. There had to be a question about what God was doing.

I've questioned. I've wondered. Surely you have as well.

Abraham, despite his struggles, held out hope. He looked at all that was against him - his aging body, his wife's aging body, the mistakes he made. He doubted, he failed, he picked himself up and moved forward toward completion. He put one foot in front of the other and made it through to the other side. And verse 22 tells us that it was credited to him as righteousness, not because he didn't struggle with his faith but because he did...and his faith was made stronger.

But that's not even the best part! Look at verse 23:

> *The words "it was credited to him" were written not for him alone, but also for us, to whom God will credit righteousness—for us who believe in him who raised Jesus our Lord from the dead. Romans 4:23-24 NIV*

So, not only did Abraham fulfill God's purpose for his life, this story, those words were put there for ME AND YOU. So we too could know that when we doubt and when we fail we can keep putting one foot in front of the other, we can keep holding out hope, and we will get through the other side with strengthened faith...and it will be credited to us as righteousness. God does not set us up for failure, He sets us up for righteousness. That righteousness comes through personal change, and that change is not always welcomed on our part.

So much can change in three years. The picture that popped up in my memories was the whole family celebrating the Christmas season in Downtown Detroit...hot cocoa in hand, warm hats on heads. Life seemed simpler, less complicated. What I wouldn't give to be back in the cold wind at Campus Martius that night, watching the skaters...listening to the sound of the Christmas music. What I wouldn't give for one more chance to try to get through to him, my son. I scanned our faces...all of them...for any sign of the coming trials that would rock my world. Nothing was there. I had no clue, no indication of what was lurking just out ahead... waiting to try to steal my joy, take my peace. But those trials also didn't know what they would be up against. They didn't know that I'm a fighter...that my joy would not be given up without a battle. Those trials didn't know that my peace was something I would learn to war for. I was badly bruised at first that year, knocked down at seemingly every turn. Unsure of how to wield my weapon, it was awkward in my hand.

One would think that since I had been reading the Word for so long I would have been better prepared. But truth be told, real-life experience is the best teacher of all. I was schooled. Over time that weapon became a part of me. It became as natural as something I had been born with. But sometimes, even our own bodies don't want to cooperate. Sometimes I was tired and it felt too heavy to lift. I would rather have stayed in bed pretending the world didn't exist. Yet God never left me there, wallowing in my own pity. He gently, yet firmly pushed me out with the words of His people, the lyrics of His songs, the Word itself in my hand. Oh, how I wish I could say I have retired my weapon, that the battle is over and done. I cannot, not yet. You can still find me on my knees, sword in hand, warring to keep my peace and regain my child...and laughing. Yes, laughing. Because the trials that set out to steal my joy did not win. I know what lies ahead in the end, even if I don't know what lies ahead tomorrow. I am clothed with strength and dignity and I can laugh at the days to come (Proverbs 31:25). But the memories of that Christmas were a stark opposition to the current Christmas season. I didn't know at the time but there was an oppression that had settled over me as 2018 was preparing to close.

I had been listening to Beth Moore's teaching series "The Present".

I had even posted it in my ladies Bible Study page because I know this time of year people can become weary. My heart had been heavy, and the extra weight had made it difficult to keep up with my normal pace. Ministry is always busier during the holidays, but this season had brought with it some additional burdens. I lost several members of my worship team to another ministry. I knew it would be good for them and for that church...but it still left a burden I had to carry in that moment. The larger burden...trial really...was the silence from Branden. If the pain of his choices hadn't been difficult enough, he had decided that he didn't want to talk to me. Most days I only thought about it on and off. But some days my heart couldn't shake it. I knew God was working. I trust Him. But some days are harder than others. This particular Sunday, I didn't have to be at our main church location, I wasn't leading worship or producing. So, I went to our second campus to see how things were going there. It's a little country community about 40 minutes from my house. While I was there I had an opportunity to hug and pray with one of our worship leaders. She's seventeen. She is the only Christian in her family. She loves Jesus and passionately worships Him. I count it an honor to help lead her. On my way out her pastor, my friend, thanked me for being an Influence in her life. I breathed it in, it was good for my soul. Once back in the car I put part three of The Present on and listened on my way home. Beth was speaking right to my heart. I had to pause it when I got home. Once inside I got busy with settling in. I opened Facebook and saw a post from the mom of seventeen and nineteen year old brothers who attend youth group with my younger children. She posted a thank you on my timeline for loving and leading her boys. It was beautiful and I was so touched. I put my headphones back on to finish part three and at the end of that teaching when there were about five minutes left, Beth started talking about how sweet God is. How He knows when we're hurting and He presents Himself to us in those moments. Beth told a story...she said that she received a tweet when she was bloody, battered and bruised. And honestly, that's how I felt that morning... how I felt when I got in my car to drive to our little country campus. That's how I felt as I stood there worshipping, feeling like my chest was wide-open...how I felt as I put my arms around that worship leader and hugged her and prayed over her. Right in the middle of that, I felt like I just needed to be done, not with life of course, but with ministry, like maybe my time had come to be done. But isn't it just like God to speak through the people around us? And isn't it just like me to need someone like Beth to point it out? In her story, she shared about an 83 year-old woman with Alzheimer's who when asked who loves her responded with Beth's name. Beth shared how God showed her that right when she most needed it. At that moment, I knew that sweet worship leader, and her pastor, and that mom of those boys said what they said the moment they said it because it was God speaking to my heart. Then He tied it all up with the bow of Beth's teaching to encourage me. I'm not too old, I'm not too tired, I'm not too used up and it hasn't been too long. God still loves me and still wants to use me even when things don't seem to be going the way I think they should. When my adult son won't even speak to me God shows me how my younger children love Him and how they serve Him and it brings hope for what lies ahead. He shows me the love of the young people He has allowed me to lead to Him, lives changed, seeds sown, and it's like a salve for my heart. He is so good, so sweet, so loving and so powerful. Maybe I could survive another Christmas in ministry (it's really not that bad...lol), maybe I would be okay again soon. Did you catch that? I'd be okay again soon. You will be okay again soon. And you are not the only one who finds yourself going back down that path again. It is normal. You are normal. Don't give up. Great things are ahead. The close of that year brought some pretty great things for me.

I had decided to ponder what I was grateful for. I had decided to focus on the incredible blessings God had given me. I wrote a couple of blogs about my kids. I wrote these blogs just before God blessed me with an incredible Christmas gift I didn't even know I wanted, so I want to share the blogs with you before moving on.

The ballerina on the tree caught my eye. She was poised so perfectly in front of the twinkling white lights. She serves as a reminder. Not so much about dancing, but more so about love. She was a gift to my daughter from a little girl she babysat. They danced together all the time. Amelia loved her, and she loved Amelia. She was a foster child and has since gone home to her biological family. But those memories will always be held dear.

For me, the ballerina stirs gratitude in my heart. Gratitude for a daughter who loves freely, and serves with an open heart and open hands. She does it without telling, so I didn't realize the depth at first. The full realization came when I was leaving the auditorium at church one Sunday during the second service. Amelia teaches a class of younger students during first service. But during second service, as I walked past the tables in the hallway, I saw her there. She was sitting with a younger girl, 9 years old. Their Bibles were open on the table. They had a devotion book and journals open as well. I don't think Amelia even knew I was there. All of her attention was on this little girl. It was a beautiful sight...her pouring into a hurting heart, showing her the love of Christ. I'm thankful, so very thankful I get to be her mom. I'm so very thankful God gives me glimpses of her heart and His hand on her life. These moments are a gift. My children are a gift. This morning I am thanking the giver.

My heart swelled with joy at what God had done, A few days later I wrote again...

His expression was one of constant delight. His flowy blonde hair and deep blue eyes could draw anyone in. He carried with him a fire for life. He had been born prematurely, and was small for most of his childhood, but that never stopped him from taking on life in a big way. I have always admired his ability to believe he can do anything. I mean, what twelve-year-old kid starts an organization to benefit the police? Or one day decides he wants to be a vlogger...and then does it? Sometimes I wonder what my life would have been like if I'd have had a fraction of the confidence he has.

Now, when I look at him I no longer see that wide-eyed innocence. His energy doesn't run wild anymore. Now there's a focus, a purpose taking shape. I am watching the boy become a man. And I am so proud of the man he is becoming.

I didn't think I could do this...raise children. I thought my heart had been broken beyond that ability. I was afraid. But God is quite clear that there isn't any fear in love. No, His perfect love casts out all fear. So with confidence, I can let him step out into this adventure called life. To try his hand at whatever catches his heart. To run and fly and be. Because this confidence is not in him, and it is not in me, but rather in the God who is in him.

And the words written in Judges 2:10 will not haunt me. As history has recorded, "...there arose another generation after them who did not know the Lord..." But not here, not today. Because he knows. There's a faith in him that tells me that he knows. There's a joy in him that tells me that he knows. There's a steady, strong confidence in him that tells me that he knows. And I am so very thankful.

My heart began to shift, to find gratitude in the midst of the craziness of the season. I'd been asked the question several times. "What do you want for Christmas?" I didn't know.

And I didn't know that I didn't know.

I didn't know until the tears began to fall...until the notification popped up on my phone...until the words were on the page in front of me.

The unheard of had become my normal. It was just normal that I hadn't heard from him for months before his most recent incarceration. It was normal that he didn't reach out to me once he was in custody. It was normal to have a child in jail. It was normal that my letters to him had gone with no response. It was normal that my prayers for him were for God to rescue his soul, no matter how. This was my new normal. And I had settled in.

I didn't know that buried beneath my faith and my hope for the future was what I wanted for Christmas this year. To hear from him, just once, to know he was okay, to know he knew I loved him.

But God knew. And in the moments of gratitude for what I had been given, in the quiet times of thanking God for the kids I do get to see every day, for the laughter I get to experience with them, He heard the deepest desire I could not even express.

And on the busiest week of my year, when the weight of ministry felt like it was too much to carry, when I just wanted to get through the week so I could rest...He showed up with a gift.

It wasn't in a box. It didn't have a bow. It was honestly bitter sweet. And I cried. I cried tears of pain, relief, joy and gratitude...all at once. Over a quarter of a page email I thought I'd never get.

Because He is the best gift giver of all. He gave me my son for Christmas this year, so I could sleep a little better in the nights to come. And He gave His Son on the first ever Christmas so I could be with Him in eternity. Not at all an even exchange, but He says I have no debt. He says I'm free.

There's nothing I could ever give back that would express my gratitude. But I'll continue to live my life trying. Will you? Can you? Can you find the place of gratitude for the gifts He's already given? Will they be enough?

"So do not be afraid of them, for there is nothing concealed that will not be disclosed, or hidden that will not be made known." Matthew 10:26

CHAPTER SIX

With that darkness looking over me and trying to settle in, I found myself praying and seeking God more than usual as 2018 was nearing its end. As I prayed and asked for direction I began to see more "spiders", or long-buried issues, that I needed to deal with. With that came the questioning of whether or not I should still be in ministry. I mean, the previous few years had been difficult, perhaps God was trying to tell me I just shouldn't be doing this anymore. I was becoming more and more convinced that my time had come to a close. I was so deeply burdened, but couldn't pinpoint exactly what it was. I made the decision to do a fast to close out the year. I picked a 48 hour time period where I would do a full fast with only water and black coffee - I couldn't see myself focusing on prayer with a headache from the caffeine withdrawal. So, the coffee had to be included. That may be an issue to take up at another time, haha.

Truth be told, the closer I get to Fifty the more I wonder if I'm done being used by God. But that thought never brings a sweet release. It is always accompanied by an unsettled spirit. Surely this can't be it. Surely my story cannot be over. I didn't come this far to sit down and die. I didn't come this far to close the book. When I said I would leave this life with guns blazing and a wagon full of souls I meant it. Somehow retiring from worship ministry and staying home just doesn't seem to fit that vision.

Many years ago I felt that God was speaking to my heart that one day I would be a teacher. One day I would write and speak publicly. I never really talked about it openly because it seems so trite. Surely I would come across as ridiculous and crazy if I let this be known. So, I didn't. I mean, eventually, I told my sister and a close girlfriend. The response from both women was so encouraging. My sister specifically told me she has always seen me that way. Wow. She saw me that way when I couldn't. God shows us to others how He sees us. I love that. At this point, I had already started writing this book but still had no idea if or how I would even complete it. I had been carrying with me a conversation I had with someone I really respect. They expressed, in a nutshell, that I cannot teach because I am too feminine to do so. The explanation of that statement isn't really important, what matters is that I took it to heart. This conversation actually took place just a short time before I told my sister about this desire deep inside to write and speak. We had been laying on the beach in Alabama, just enjoying the sunshine and the sister-to-sister conversation when I told her. It was one of those moments where I knew God was there, in the midst of the conversation. He was hearing my heart and responding in His goodness. We later were looking through some shops and I came across a cross made of freshwater pearls. It was so beautiful; so fragile, yet so strong. It was like God was talking to me through this cross...telling me that this thing that represented the greatest sacrifice, the only thing to overcome death itself, was still powerful even though it was covered in something as beautiful and feminine as pearls. My packaging doesn't change the power of the message I bring. God actually created me with His own hands. He made me feminine, He made me silly and funny and loud. He is not surprised by the girlie things I love or by the kind of crazy I tend to be. In fact, He made me this way totally on purpose, so I can reach specific people who will hear from me what they will not hear from others. And yes, I know that we all have things that need to change. Believe me, I've been changing since the day I met Him. But the basics of who I am were very intentional on my Creator's part. That goes for you too. Do not forget it. Do not allow others to make you think that you are not enough, or that you are too much. You are exactly who God made you to be. We all need a little refining...but He loves who you are. As I held that beautiful cross in my hand I knew I had to buy it to commemorate this day, this moment, when God said I am exactly what He wants me to be. It hangs on the wall in my stairwell with the ever-growing collection of crosses that commemorate important moments in my life. I see it every single day. It reminds me to keep walking toward the goal.

Yet, there I was at the close of the year still questioning what He was calling me to. As I was preparing for my fast I felt as though God was telling me to go back and listen again to another Beth Moore teaching series I had just finished up. It was called Advance. My fast began on the morning of December 28th. As soon as I started listening to Beth that morning I knew that Advance was my word for the coming year. I have never really been that person who does that, you know, has a word for the year. I always feel like it's a little corny. But I know God's voice - most times - and this time I was sure. So, I wrote it down. Advance. That was my word. As Beth taught, she shared that she had written down every single Scripture with the word advance in it. One of the Scriptures she shared wasn't really a part of her teaching, but I knew immediately it was mine. Jeremiah 46:3 "Prepare buckler and shield and advance into battle." I wrote it down. Then I began to dig into what the words in the Scripture mean. I read the story behind it, I studied it and I meditated on it to let God speak something new to my heart. And boy did He ever speak to my heart. I was like a starving animal devouring every letter, every word on the page. I wanted to be fed and through the feeding to be changed. I soon discovered that a buckler and a shield are both used to protect warriors in battle. But as warriors, we have to choose one or the other because we cannot carry both and still wield our sword. So we either choose the shield which is worn on the arm and easily mobile, used to ward off arrows and attacks from afar; or we choose the buckler which is used in hand to hand, up close combat and often can be used to disarm the enemy. Both are useful, both are effective, so how do we choose? Especially when we don't even know what kind of attack is coming our way. I was perplexed by this. And in the midst of my questioning and searching,

I saw it. Right there in Psalm 91 verse 4.

He will cover you with his pinions and under his wings you will find refuge, his faithfulness is a shield and buckler.

His faithfulness is our shield AND our buckler! We don't have to choose one or the other because He is going to be both for us. And as a side note, time and time again in the Bible we see God's hand being called mighty and HIs arm being called strong. He can surely guard us. His arm will never tire of holding the shield and His hand never tire of disarming our enemy with the buckler. Our strength cannot compare. So, if He is bearing the buckler and the shield what do we do? We advance. Not only do we advance, but we advance into battle. What is the definition of advance? To move forward purposefully, to cause progress! I knew that God was telling me to finish this book, this one right here, the one you are reading right now. Every ounce of fear was gone. I had no reason to be afraid of failure. He is my buckler and shield, I just need to advance. I was keenly aware that the advance of writing this book would bring on the advance of speaking, and in it all, God is going to use my story to set people free. You, my son, anyone I can reach. Why? I know you know. Because nothing is wasted. Not one thing is wasted. Not one single moment. I will never have to ask, "What was it all for?" I already know! For His glory!

So, that was how I ended out the year, 2018. I finished my fast with a journal full of notes and entered 2019 feeling as though the oppression I carried had been lifted. I was ready. Ready for whatever God had in store for me. Yet, I was sure He was still speaking to me, still trying to get something through. I remember the days when God would pursue me openly and publicly. It's not really like that anymore. At first, I didn't understand. I thought He was hiding, being silent. Then I realized that our relationship has grown. It's not that He doesn't pursue me. Our relationship is different now. Similar to the changes that happen in a marriage.

He speaks to me in private. His Word has become our dialogue. It's deeper and sweeter than ever. This is the progression of a life lived for Him. We go from being chased to chasing His plan. But I was aware that He was once again openly pursuing me as I entered 2019. He was talking to me any way He could get my attention. I felt an urgency to go where I could meet with Him. I had been on Facebook and saw a post a friend of mine shared. There was going to be a worship night at a church about 40 minutes from me. I knew I had to go. I didn't know anyone that attended that church, and I knew I could "be alone" with God even in a room with a bunch of other people. No one would know me. On the drive that night I worshiped in the car, I prayed and told God that I couldn't wait to just worship Him. I let Him know that even if He didn't speak to my heart that night, I was going to pour my love out for HIm.

I wasn't surprised at all, however, that He did speak to me. He did. We worshiped for two hours. TWO WHOLE HOURS. It was like a river in a dry and crusty desert. It was everything my tired soul needed. I sang and prayed and poured myself out. And I was alone with Him. At the end of the night the pastor spoke, just briefly, but he shared three words....bereavement, birthing and building. It was like an imprint in my own personal timeline. God had already told me to advance. To move forward and make progress. To stop waiting for Him to move for me. But I clearly saw that I had been grieving for so long, I had been hurting for so long, and my season of bereavement was coming to a close. That is not to say that there wouldn't be more challenges ahead in regard to my son. There will be. His story is not over, and neither is mine. But the bereavement season I've been in is coming to a close. God is birthing something in me. He is birthing this book. In the teaching series I listened to by Beth Moore she said, "There is a you that you have not yet met". Write that down girlfriend! There is a you that you have not yet met! You definitely want to meet her! I wrote it down in my journal. God is birthing that me right now. And the next season of my life will be the building of what God has called me into. I won't be building it, He will. But I have to take the steps He leads me to take. I have to move when He says move. By the way, the struggle I had been having over whether or not to stay in ministry,...God also made it clear that I am to stay put until He says otherwise. Sometimes He will show us things long before they come to pass.

Honestly, my head was sort of spinning from all of the things God was downloading to my heart. But He wasn't yet finished. I was listening to Michael Todd on the treadmill the day after the worship night. I listen to him every week. The first teaching I had ever heard by him was in January 2018. It was their vision series for that year. I had the privilege of listening every week as God grew that church in incredible ways. So, there I was, on the treadmill listening to the vision series for 2019. Shortly into the teaching I had this stirring in me that what was being spoken was for me. I know, I know, I felt the same way, like "Yeah, okay Libbie. It's all for you". Believe me, I felt that way. I actually spoke out loud to myself, "Why do you think everything is about you????" This church is in Oklahoma! You are in MIchigan! This is not about you! The word he shared that would be their word for 2019 is Release, and in his teaching, he talked about all the different types of releasing God was leading us to do. Yes, he did talk about people releasing the book God gave them. I still kept telling myself that teaching was not for me. I could not bring myself to believe that I am that important to God. I could not bring myself to accept that He would speak to me through Beth Moore, and then a pastor I don't even know at a worship night, and then Michael Todd. I don't show up like that on God's radar. But then....then...he got to the end of his teaching and shared this Scripture from Luke:

The Spirit of the Sovereign Lord is on me, because the Lord has anointed me to proclaim good news to the poor. He has sent me to bind up the brokenhearted, to proclaim freedom for the captives and release from darkness for the prisoners, to proclaim the year of the Lord's favor and the day of vengeance of our God, to com-

fort all who mourn, and provide for those who grieve in Zion—to bestow on them a crown of beauty instead of ashes, the oil of joy instead of mourning, and a garment of praise instead of a spirit of despair. They will be called oaks of righteousness, a planting of the Lord for the display of his splendor.

No big deal, right? I mean, it's a great Scripture, but what does that have to do with me? Good God, I could shout just typing this out right now. Honestly, no lie, I wrote this exact Scripture out in my journal, except from Isaiah 61 back in January 2018 as my own life mission statement. At that moment he may as well have said, "Libbie Hall, I'm talking to you." It was like he addressed it right to me. I was so overwhelmed. I knew that 2019 was my year to advance, to move forward out of the pain and into the calling He had ahead of me.

So, again, why am I telling you this? To brag about how God talks to me? Nope. Look at this Scripture in Joshua 4:14,

That day the Lord exalted Joshua in the sight of all Israel; and they stood in awe of him all the days of his life, just as they had stood in awe of Moses.

The people were in awe of Joshua and Moses because they both heard God's voice as He directed them for the people. Sometimes people are in awe of others who hear God, who are close to Him and get answers and direction. But that privilege is for everyone. It is for me and it is for YOU. When we receive Christ we receive the Holy Spirit. The Bible says He is our counselor. We have to develop our hearing, no doubt, but that relationship needs to be tended to. And when it is developed we learn to hear His voice. It took Joshua 40 years in the wilderness. We are privileged for sure...on this side of the resurrection. We enjoy a relationship they didn't know back then. He literally lives in us. He speaks to us. This whole chapter has been one example after another of how He will use others to speak...but most often all we have to do is open up the letter He wrote to us, the Bible. He speaks in volumes there. He is speaking to you right now. He is leading, directing, informing...develop your hearing. Open the Bible, read, read again. Worship, and then worship some more. Cut the noise of the world out and turn Him up. Nothing will ever be the same.

"How you respond to the enemy of your soul determines whether his plan for your life or God's plan for your life is realized." Stormie Omartian

CHAPTER SEVEN

It's March 2019 and my story hasn't changed much. It's cold and dreary this morning. And I'm tired of the long cold winter. "Doing" just feels hard right now. And without invitation grief showed up today...in the form of a letter from my son. Maybe the winter welcomed grief in, I'm not sure. But the letter was the door I opened. Don't get me wrong, his words were nice. He shared information and thoughts...there was sadness mixed in. He shared about a friend who overdosed in the program he will be entering soon. His heart hurt over it. It was a reminder to me of the world my son lives in. It's a world so distant from mine...yet I could get there right outside of my door if I chose to. I haven't been there in a while. I only visited before Branden was incarcerated. I would go to see him, to try to bring him out. It never worked.

I remember him telling me a couple of years ago that life is dark. He went on about how bad and negative it is. I let him talk for a while and when he was done I gently shared a different view. I tried to present a different window through which he could look. Because I know his reality hasn't always been what it is now. I know the family he grew up with, the people who have always loved him. I know the sporting events we never missed...the school activities we all attended...the holidays we celebrated together. I was there. I know. I know that the darkness that engulfed him hasn't always been there. I know that his brother and sister have never felt that kind of darkness....and there was a time when he hadn't either. I also know it's hard to find the way out. But there is indeed a way.

I also know that I can't force him to walk into a different reality.

It's a choice he will have to make. I pray every day that he makes it. I speak life and truth over him and trust the God who calls him son. Branden was His son before he was mine.

The "doing" is hard today. Even though God Himself had revived my heart, even though I have been encouraged and built up. This is a day when the "doing" is hard. But I will choose to do anyway...because Branden needs someone pulling for him...Amelia and Wyatt need an example of how to stay in the light. They all need someone pointing them to the Father...so hope doesn't die and the darkness doesn't win.

The darkness doesn't win.

I have a Facebook friend whose son committed suicide a few years ago. He was a talented young man. He went to church, but his struggle was heavy. She posts old videos of him playing and singing all the time. My heart breaks for her. Recently she posted that someone asked her when she was going to move on. What? I'm sorry, what? When is she going to move on? She lost a child. She will never move on. There will be days when the grief is at bay...when she will laugh and not think about her son every moment. But there will be days, like the one above, when grief knocks on her door early in the morning. And even if she doesn't open it, grief will find its way in, through a window or a crack in the wall. And she will be unable to deny that it is there. Who are we to deny her those moments? Who are we to question her walk? I pray for her, that she will understand who she is in Christ, and that she will let God use that pain for His glory. That seems impossible, doesn't it? That God could use the pain of losing a child for His glory? His Word says that He will make beauty from our ashes. He will, but we have to give Him the ashes. He will take even the most horrible of situations and use them to lead someone else to Him. Nothing wasted, right? Nothing.

Don't be afraid to let others see your pain. Don't be afraid to let God use it to touch lives. We only have this one chance. The years

65

fly by quickly. One day you will be like me, looking in the mirror wondering if you can still be used. As long as there is breath in your lungs you can be used. In fact, if there is breath in your lungs He is most definitely not done with you yet! When He is done with you there will be no more breath. You will find yourself before the throne in heaven...and oh that you would hear, "Well done good and faithful servant."

At some point during the process of struggle and gaining peace I started another women's Bible study. I have had studies before and have handed them off to someone else to lead as things in my life got busier.

But this time felt different. I can't say exactly how. These women felt closer, my heart seemed to be tied to theirs in a different sort of way. In the past my groups always used a book, but this time I was bringing studies God had given me in my prayer time. So that was different too. It just felt deeper somehow.

And so we dug in. We began to study women in the Bible, generational differences, the Holy Spirit, faith. I've watched them struggle with their own faith and ask some hard questions. I've watched them find healing for wounded souls and discover that God wants to use them. There's a fulfillment and a joy in this that I just can't explain.

They have seen me walk through some hard stuff. They've prayed for my children and I have prayed for theirs. They have seen the struggle and heard the laughter. We've shared tears of both kinds. This is the good stuff. It really is. This is what God wants to do with our pain. He wants to create a work of art from it. One that can be shared with the people around us so they too can find themselves made whole. So they too can love and give and lead people to Him.

I am currently preparing our next study. It's on living with Intention. I'm figuring out that this is my intentional living. This right here. Meeting with these women, writing this book, homeschooling my kids, and loving my husband. Why do we think it has to be something grandiose? Why do we complicate it? I think it all comes down to two Scriptures.

Jesus replied: " 'Love the Lord your God with all your heart and with all your soul and with all your mind.' And the second is like it: 'Love your neighbor as yourself.'
Matthew 22:37, -39 NIV

Therefore go and make disciples of all nations, baptizing them in the name of the Father and of the Son and of the Holy Spirit, and teaching them to obey everything I have commanded you. And surely I am with you always, to the very end of the age."
Matthew 28:19-20 NIV

Do you see it? We are to love God and let that love flow outward to everyone else to the point where we want to introduce them to Him. Like, love Him and them so much that we can't wait for them to meet. Have you ever had two friends that didn't know each other, but they were both so awesome? You loved being with them both and thought about how amazing it would be if you could all hang out together? It's like that! You love God with all you are. And now you love all the people and just want everyone to know each other and love each other too!

When everything we do in life points back to the two Scriptures above we are living with intention. I think the mistake some people make is to think that in order to live for Him we have to 1) have it all together and 2) be a missionary or a Pastor. But that is so far off the mark. In order to live for Him we just need to ...live for Him.

I just had coffee with a sweet young friend who works in an environment that is not very Christian friendly. The people are great and she loves her job, but they do not have a positive view of Christianity in general. She was sharing with me how she doesn't purposely talk about Jesus at work, but somehow people began asking her about what she believes. She doesn't feel as though she is serving God well. But as we talked I was so excited about what she was telling me! In living out her daily life she is showing who Jesus is. She is loving and caring and hard working. And they now want to know what she has that they don't! So they are asking, and now she can respond. And she does, she simply tells them what they want to know. Man, this situation couldn't be any more perfect! She is living out the great commission every day.

That is intentional living. We need to let people see the real us. The messy, broken, joyful, peaceful, loving us...and when they ask why...or how or who...we simply point to Him.

It's true, my story hasn't changed much, but I have. I guess that's really why I wrote this book. I wanted you to see that we all have struggles, we all deal with pain. At some point in every person's life, they will face something that makes them feel as though they can't go on. But there is hope. I want you to see the hope. I want you to know that there is always good mixed in with the bad...even when we can't see it. I want you to know that you are not alone, that you are loved and that He has a purpose and a plan for you.

No one wants to be a villain in anyone else's story. But truth be told we all are. Every one of us. We have all been the bad guy to someone else, even if we didn't mean to be.

CHAPTER EIGHT

I was reminded today of a prayer I prayed some time ago. It was back when we had bailed Branden out of jail in preparation for rehab. The circumstances when he ran were not good, and he was angry at us. The plan was that my husband would drive the two hours to get him, then another hour and a half to a rehab center where Branden had an appointment, and then another hour and a half to come home. But when Branden got in the car he was very obstinate and a terrible argument between him and my husband took place. Branden exited the vehicle and that was the last time I saw him. I talked to him a couple more times, and then he basic-ally stopped responding to me. There were a few months when I didn't even know if he was alive. At times my heart was gripped with fear. I prayed constantly. One prayer went something like this, "Lord, if he never speaks to me again I will be okay, will You please just rescue him?" I was willing to bear the pain of losing him from my life, I just wanted to know that I would see him in eternity.

A few months later he was picked up and had been in jail ever since. As I discussed earlier, he did start writing back to me, but then suddenly the responses stopped. Eventually, the app I was using couldn't even locate him to send letters anymore. So I waited...and waited.

Then, I found out that he had been released on probation a few weeks earlier and chose to not reach out to me. My step Mom talked to him and he said he just wasn't ready to forgive us. How-ever, he had been going to church with his father and was living clean. He was working every day and planning on going back to school. These are all things I've prayed for. Yet my heart could not rejoice in it. It was just heavy and felt wounded. I prayed and stood in faith, believing for his life, his soul. And there I was with the wrong end of this situation facing me. I felt angry and hurt at the thought of the years of laboring in prayer for him, the sleepless nights, the constant developing of my faith in order to just function in the midst of the pain. Yet, the truth is that God answered my prayer. Branden is clean and is going to church....not with me...but he is going. So, now, I am asking God to help me to be grateful. I'm thanking Him for answering my prayer, even though it hurts. And in the middle of it all, I know that the story is not over yet. I've gotten pretty good at managing the pain, I can move on with life and lay it all at His feet. Once again He has shown me that He is good. Once again, I can see that trusting Him is the best way, the only way.

We are getting on a plane soon. A much-needed break is coming once again. We are headed back to California where I grew up. I always feel like a child when I'm there. Simply being there brings so many memories I don't really want to remember. But they are there. Waiting for me to look them in the face again. It's an opportunity for me to remember just how far I've come...just how good my God is. He is so, so very good.

This book, from one chapter to the next, may feel like a roller coaster. Seriously, you probably wondered how in the world I can get through a day with so many struggles. But stop and think for a moment. I mean, you probably do not have an incarcerated child. But surely, most people reading this book have faced tragedy of some sort in life. Surely you too find grief at your door from time to time. Surely, you have days where you sit, staring out your window wondering how you will find the strength to face the world. And yet, here you are. You did it, another day. And the truth is that most of life is wonderful. These stories took place over a four year time period. They are just selected moments that I felt I needed to share. I mentioned in an earlier chapter that I love to laugh. I really do. I laugh every single day. I laugh with my kids constantly. I laugh at myself, I laugh at them, I laugh at the world. And like I said, one day all the videos my kids have taken of me laughing will be cut together and played at my funeral. Why? Because that is how I want to be remembered. Joyful, laughing so hard that tears roll down my face. My life is incredibly joyful. I know that may be hard to really grasp after reading so much of my pain. But truly, the joy outweighs the pain. I struggled with whether or not I should be open about the pain I face in life. I do not want to point to it all the time. I don't want anyone to think that's what life is. But at the same time, I want you to know the pain you face is normal. It is a part of this life. You are not alone. Most people do not live lives that are all pink and perfect. Most people also live in darker hues and realities that are far from perfection. But when you know Jesus, really know Him, joy is inevitable. When you begin to understand who you are and what you were made to do your joy will far outweigh your pain as well. My hope is that you will see my struggles, and see how I learned to overcome them, and you too will take up your sword and fight.

And now I lay by the pool at my step dad's house. Over a year has passed since my mother's death. He moved into a new home to soften the pain of the memories that surrounded him. The new house was much like the one they lived in when Branden was a baby. As I lay in the quiet, the sun soaking into my skin, I can see him there...that little sun hat on his curly head, tiny feet stuck through the holes in the plastic floaty. He was my pride and joy. At this moment I can't help but wonder if things would be different if I could just go back. Would his life be different if I hadn't divorced his father? Or maybe if I hadn't remarried? If he had stayed the center of my world? Or maybe this is just who he would have been regardless. I don't know. I'll never know. I do know that regret and shame are heavy. Too heavy to carry into a future filled with hope. They must be checked at the door. So check them at the door. I did. And in moments of remembrance, when the weight tries to resettle in my soul I will check them again. I will choose hope over and over. Even in the midst of sorrow, even when the world looks dark, I will choose hope.

I've talked several times in this book about nothing being wasted. Jesus said those same words once. Let me show you. There is a story in the gospels about a little boy whose lunch was used to feed well over five thousand people. It was a miracle. Even the disciples were skeptics. They couldn't imagine how that small amount of food would be enough to feed all of the people who had come out to hear Jesus preach. After everyone ate from just a couple loaves of bread and a few fish Jesus said to them, "Gather the fragments so that nothing is wasted." and they picked up baskets full of leftovers, enough to feed many, many more.

Is your life fragmented? Your heart? Gather those up because Jesus Is not about to waste it. No, He wants to use it to feed a hurting, dying, hungry world. Decide today...nothing wasted. Decide before you close this book...nothing wasted. Did grief show up this morning? It will not be wasted. Did shame try to pay a visit this week? It will not be wasted. Give it all to Jesus and watch what He will do. Keep hoping against hope, believing through unbelief, swinging your sword. Nothing will be wasted.

weight tries to resettle in my soul I will check them again.

HEARTFELT THANKS!!!

Thank you to Mitzi Hollins for editing this book. Your grammatical giftedness is a blessing to me!

Thank you to all of my friends who read this book and gave input before it launched. You are greatly appreciated!

Thank you Mom, Dad, Brian, Amelia and Wyatt for your love and support and for making my life so much fun! I love you.

Made in the USA
Monee, IL
23 November 2019